THE COMPLETE
BEGINNER'S GUIDE
TO MAKING
AND FLYING KITES

THE COMPLETE BEGINNER'S GUIDE TO MAKING AND FLYING KITES

By Edward F. Dolan, Jr.

Illustrated by John Lane

DOUBLEDAY & COMPANY, INC., GARDEN CITY, NEW YORK

This book is for Richard B. Lyttle.
He thought it was a good idea.

LIBRARY OF CONGRESS CATALOGING IN PUBLICATION DATA

DOLAN, EDWARD F
  THE COMPLETE BEGINNER'S GUIDE TO MAKING AND FLYING KITES.

    BIBLIOGRAPHY: P. 145
    INCLUDES INDEX.
    SUMMARY: AN INTRODUCTION TO THE CONSTRUCTION AND FLYING OF KITES INCLUDING DISCUSSIONS OF VARIOUS FLAT, BOW, AND BOX KITES.
    1. KITES. [1. KITES] I. LANE, JOHN, 1932. II. TITLE.
TL759.D64   796.1'5
LIBRARY OF CONGRESS CATALOG CARD NUMBER 75–36585
ISBN 0-385-04905-6 TRADE
    0-385-04937-4 PREBOUND

CONTENTS

1

YOU AND YOUR KITE

Oh, to break the bonds of Earth;
To rise, soaring, with the bird;
To lie, reclined, among the clouds;
To see the land from high,
From higher than the highest mountain.
It is the cherish'd dream
Of cherish'd dreams.

ANONYMOUS

These words speak of one of man's oldest urges—the urge to fly. It is the urge that gave us the balloon, the glider, the dirigible, the airplane, and the space vehicle. And it is the urge that, long before any of the above marvels ever took shape, gave us that fascinating flying machine of sticks and paper—the kite.

For at least thirty centuries now, the kite has captivated man as it dances at the end of a string and enables him to taste the wonder of flight without ever taking his feet off the ground. He has sailed it aloft to frighten away evil spirits or to bring his loved ones good fortune. He has fished with it and used it to pull his sailing ships from windless harbors. He has tied meteorological instruments to it for his weather studies. He has sat in a sling below it and has floated to heights of more than one hundred feet, an activity that helped pave the way to powered flight. And throughout all the centuries, he has released it skyward in a variety of shapes and sizes for the sheer fun of it all.

Fun. That word brings us right to you. You've probably already flown your share of kites, all of them inexpensively purchased at a hobby shop, the dime store, or the grocery store. Perhaps you've even made a kite or two. Homemade or "store bought," they've given you a few hours of pleasure out in the open during the breezy times of year. But have you ever thought of kiting as a full-fledged, year-round hobby?

Have you, for instance, ever thought of building a whole collection of kites—kites of all shapes and sizes, kites from all parts of the world, kites developed in our own time, and kites ancient in origin? Have you ever thought of designing your own kites? Or of how best to fly a kite? Or of flying it in a train or in tandem? Or of the attachments—messengers, parachutes, and gliders—that can add so much to the fun? Or of the aerial games that can be played? Or of the competitions that can be held?

If so, you've been on the threshold of a hobby that has long delighted thousands of people of all ages, of all walks of life, of all nationalities. The whole purpose of this book is to help you step across that threshold and get in on all the fun. Once in kiting, you'll find it is a hobby that is also a sport, a hobby that can be enjoyed practically all year long, one that can be mingled with other hobbies, and one that can entertain you endlessly for little or no money.

All this is really saying a mouthful. But it's all true.

Try running your kite up through a tricky ground wind until it catches the true wind above. Coax your kite out of a layer of dead air and into a lively one. Go after a record altitude run. Send ten kites up in a train. Work to bring an unruly kite head-up and into the wind. Challenge a friend to an aerial duel. Try any of these things and you'll know that you've got a sport on your hands.

Or just stand there, flying your kite and enjoying the great outdoors, breathing in the good clean air, and feeling the sun on your face. If your flying ground is out in the country, try hiking or cycling there. Take a picnic lunch along. Watch the nature around you and get acquainted with it. With friends, try an evening flight, tent down for the night, and then greet the new day with a dawn flight. Or try fishing with your kite.

Doesn't all this add up to hiking, cycling, camping, and nature study—all rolled into one?

Indeed, kiting *is* a sport. But what about the claim that it can be enjoyed practically all year round?

Granted, kiting has a season—the windy weeks from late February to early April. But you needn't store your kites for the rest of the year. They aren't able to read a calendar, and so they'll go happily aloft on any day of the year when there is a breeze blowing at a velocity somewhere above a very gentle four miles an hour.

Actually, there are only three times when your kite should be put away for the day: when there is no wind at all to support it; when the wind is over twenty miles an hour and likely to damage it; and when the weather is stormy or threatening to storm. At that time, there's the danger of lightning and an electrical charge down through the wet flying line.

So don't think that you must wait for the winds of March. Whenever the day is clear and a little breezy, out you can go to fly. And those stormy days of winter—well, wouldn't they be great times for building new kites or dreaming up new designs?

Now what of the next claim—that kiting can be mingled with other hobbies? Do you like to build model airplanes? Kite-building is a form of model-building, one in which you can further put your model-making skills to work. You may find that you'll like to trade off between the two, perhaps building one or several kites and then turning to the planes for a change of pace. And, if you happen to be an inexperienced modelmaker, you'll discover that kites are generally easier to build than model planes and ships.

Or is science your hobby? You'll be fascinated by the aerodynamic factors involved in the kite. There will be plenty to talk about at your next Science Club meeting.

Or photography? Try attaching your camera to a kite and building a collection of aerial photographs.

Or art? The kite face can easily become a new canvas for you. It lends itself to all sorts of artistic expression.

And, finally, can kiting really give you endless hours of pleasure for little or no money? Some hobbies—photography and sailing, for instance—require heavy expenditures for equipment. But kiting—well, the truth is that you can spend as little or as much money on it as you wish.

For example, you can purchase a simple kite for less than a dollar, or you can count out from five to more than seventy dollars for more extravagant models. You can fly your kite at the end of a length of household string wrapped around an old stick, or you can invest in a fancy rod-and-reel. You can build a kite with sticks and paper found around the house, or you can put your money into ready-made sticks—even fiber-glass rods—and fine papers, plastics, or cloths.

In this book, you'll find the plans for forty-five different kites. Practically all these kites can be built at no cost whatsoever if you're willing to fashion your sticks from old boards or bamboo shades and use other materials found in the house or garage. And, if you must purchase your materials, you can literally keep your costs down to next to nothing if you shop wisely and refuse to be carried away by some of the fancy items you come across. Kite materials can be among the most inexpensive found for any hobby.

In all, as one kite man has wryly put it, "Kiting can be just about as inexpensive as standing around doing nothing."

Should you decide that kiting is exactly the hobby you've been looking for, you'll find that you're engaged in a pastime that dates back at least three thousand years. It is a pastime whose history is rich in legend, tradition, pleasure, and practical accomplishment.

Many kite men like to think that the kite was born when some ancient thinker saw a leaf floating in the air and wondered if he could make it fly high by attaching a length of corded vine to it. But no one really knows when or how the kite came into being. The best guess is that it originated in China and then slowly made its way throughout the rest of Asia and into Europe.

Chinese folklore abounds with legends of the kite. For instance, an ancient military leader is said to have captured a fortress with its help. After an unsuccessful attack, he flew a kite up over the fortress walls and used the flying line to measure the distance between them and his camp. Then he ordered his troops to burrow a tunnel that distance. The soldiers emerged inside the fortress and quickly overwhelmed the surprised defenders.

Centuries later, so another story goes, an emperor cleverly employed the kite as a danger signal. Though threatened by invaders, he could not keep his troops constantly on guard since they were also farmers who tended his surrounding fields. He solved the problem by flying kites from his palace walls whenever observers sighted the enemy. On glimpsing the kites, the farmer-soldiers would drop their tools and pick up their weapons.

Traditions, as well as legends, soon surrounded the kite in China. The people took to sending their kites aloft with reeds or small harps attached so that the humming and wailing sounds would frighten away nighttime intruders and evil spirits; in fact, the Chinese term for the kite—*feng cheng*—comes from the small harps and means, literally, "wind harp." Also seeing the kite as a symbol of good luck, the people decorated it with a crane or a turtle to insure long life or shaped it as a dragon to symbolize their gratitude for a prosperous year. In one ancient ceremony, the family sent a kite far into the distance on the eldest son's seventh birthday. It was then cut free and allowed to float away, carrying with it all bad luck for the child.

Of course, the kite was also flown for pleasure. Many Chinese thought that its peaceful flight aided contemplation. All saw it as symbolic of man's ever-rising aspirations.

Wherever it went, the kite became as much a source of legend as it was in China. The Polynesians told stories of ancestors who communicated with their gods on high via the kite. The Japanese cherished the tale of the thief who rode a kite to the top of a castle in an effort to steal two ornamental fish of solid gold there. The Koreans immortalized the general whose kites inspired his troops to engage and defeat an invader force; he secretly launched a number of kites, all with lanterns attached, above his camp and then spread the word that the lights in the night sky betokened the friendship and support of the gods. The people of Crete invented the myth of Icarus, the boy who donned wings of wax and flew into the sky, coming at last so close to the sun that the wings melted and he fell to his death. Many mythologists believe that the tale stems from early Cretan efforts to use the kite for manned flight.

And in every new country, tradition joined the mounting legends. In Thailand kites were flown as decorations above the royal palace and were sent aloft to invite the speedy arrival of the monsoon season, so beneficial to the nation's farming. In Japan May 5 continues to be observed as "Boy's Festival," with the day being devoted to flying kites in honor of good sons. Prior to World War II the people on the Japanese island of Tokushima followed their old annual tradition of raising the largest kite in the world—a giant weighing 1,700 pounds and measuring sixty-five feet in diameter. Called the *Wanwan*, it was made of 2,500 sheets of paper and used ten lengths of ship's hawser, all bundled together, for a tail.

Practical work was soon added to the legends, the traditions, and the pleasures of flying. The early peoples of Malaysia and the South Pacific fished with kites made of plant leaves. Portuguese sailors of the fifteenth century sent kites up when a ship had to be pulled free of a harbor whose surrounding hills blocked off the wind. The seventeenth-century Japanese architect, Kawamura Zuiken, used kites to lift workmen to the roof of a temple under construction. In 1822 an English schoolteacher named George Pocock lashed two giant kites to a lightweight carriage of his design. The kites—one fifteen feet long in the spine, the other twelve feet—were known to tow the carriage along at speeds up to twenty miles an hour.

Here in our own country, almost a half-century before Pocock's birth, Benjamin Franklin unreeled a kite into a storm and, taking a painful shock for his trouble, proved that lightning and an electrical current are the same. The experiment marked one of the earliest scientific uses to which the kite was put. Out of the flight came new understandings of electricity and the invention of the still-in-demand lightning rod.

At about the time of Franklin's "Philadelphia experiment," as it was called, a Scottish astronomer, Dr. Alexander Wilson, determined the temperatures at higher altitudes by flying kites carrying thermometers. In the nineteenth century English meteorologist E. D. Archibald tied anemometers to kites and dispatched them to record wind speeds at various altitudes.

Some of the most interesting work with the kite was done at the turn of our century, when experiments were in full flower to satisfy that age-old craving to fly. Some men were testing balloons, gliders, and assorted "flapping wing" machines. Others were concentrating on kites able to lift a man high, hoping that such kites would help to attain an understanding of the aerodynamic factors necessary for that miracle sure to come—powered flight. Among the aeronautical pioneers working with kites were Lawrence Hargrave, B. F. S. Baden-Powell, the telephone's Alexander Graham Bell, and the Wright brothers.

Hargrave, an Australian, first tried to build "flapping wing" machines in the 1880s and then, after several disappointments, turned to the kite. He eventually designed a model that he called the "cellular kite." It could lift extremely heavy weights, and in 1894 he sat in a sling below four of his cellulars and rode them to a height of sixteen feet. He could have gone higher but, for safety's sake, decided to come back down. The cellular has been called one of the great modern innovations in kite design. Today we know it simply as the box kite.

Englishman Baden-Powell, the brother of the founder of the Boy Scouts, is credited with the development of the first truly reliable kite system for lifting a man. He designed a six-sided kite called the "levitor" (you'll have a chance to build it in Chapter 5) that, when flown in trains of four to seven, could lift a man to a height of one hundred feet or more. The "pilot" flew in a basket below the kites, with his altitude controlled by ropes extending down to a ground crew. The British government was much impressed by the levitor system and planned to use it for military observation during the Boer War. Baden-Powell and his kites— each of them thirty-six feet long—were sent to South Africa, but the fighting had ended by the time of his arrival.

For his aeronautical research, Bell developed what is known as the tetrahedral kite (you'll find it in Chapter 9). Considered as much of a design innovation as the box kite, it was constructed of sticks arranged in one or more triangular sections, called "cells." Bell began in the 1890s with a one-cell model and then gradually increased the number of cells until, in the early 1900s, he was able to build the "Cygnet" (meaning "young swan"), a monster forty feet long and containing 3,393 cells. Weighing over two hundred pounds and towed by a steamer, it carried a man 168 feet above Nova Scotia's Baddeck Bay. The tetrahedral remains a popular kite to this day for those builders who enjoy trying their hand at especially odd-shaped kites.

As for the Wrights, they were especially interested in what could be done to control an aircraft when it was struck by sudden gusts or up- and downdrafts. As they saw the problem, the pilot was helpless to do more than shift his weight and hope for the best. And so they began a study of soaring birds and soon found that such fliers as hawks and buzzards twist their wing tips to control flight. The brothers achieved a similar control in 1899 with a "warping kite," a kite whose surfaces could be changed to meet varying wind conditions. Armed with what they had learned, the Wrights then built their first "flying machines" and went on to Kitty Hawk, North Carolina, for their historic flights.

Once powered flight was here, interest in man-lifting kites dwindled. But the kite men could be content that their studies had helped pave the way to the airplane. As for the kite itself, it continued to do yeoman's duty. With a camera attached, it flew above San Francisco and took a series of historic pictures of the devastation left by the great earthquake and fire of 1906. In its box form, it was sent aloft from weather stations throughout the world to make meteorological observations, a job that it held until replaced by the airplane and the weather balloon in the 1930s. In one of its latest designs—the parawing—it has led to the development of the "flying jeep" (an experimental craft capable of hauling loads of 1,000 pounds for short distances), the para-glider for bringing astronauts back to earth, and the free-floating aircraft responsible for one of today's most popular sports—hang gliding.

But, most important of all, the kite has continued to do in our century the work that it has always done best. It has continued to bring pleasure to countless builders and fliers of all ages, of all occupations, and of all countries. Hopefully, you are the newest addition to their ranks.

If so, a hearty welcome to you.

May the kite now, as the heart of your new hobby, bring you quite as much pleasure.

2

KNOWING YOUR KITE

Perhaps you plan only to fly ready-made kites. Or perhaps you're of a mind to do your own building, starting with the kites described later in this book and eventually moving on to models of your own invention. Whatever your choice, there are certain basic facts that you need to know about the nature of the kite and its construction. They will make a better builder and flier of you, and will add much to your enjoyment by giving you a greater understanding and appreciation of the marvelous thing that is at the heart of your new hobby.

In this chapter and the next, we'll be looking at those basic facts. We'll begin with that most basic fact of all—the *why* behind the kite's ability to fly—and end with a series of tips on how the kite is best built.

Why Your Kite Flies

As is the airplane, the kite is an *aerodyne*, a heavier-than-air machine. Both defy the laws of gravity and break free of the ground by taking advantage of a scientific principle first stated by Daniel Bernoulli of Switzerland in the eighteenth century. The principle holds that when air moves quickly, its pressure decreases, but that when it moves slowly, its pressure increases.

Though the principle works for both the kite and the airplane, the kite uses it in its own way. A comparison of how the two aerodynes fly illustrates the difference.

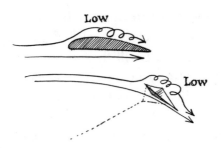

Airplane wing and kite principles of flight

The airplane, of course, derives lift from its curved-top wing. As the wing splits the air, it drives some air particles across its upper curve while sending others along its flat underside. An invisible race is triggered, with the particles on the curve accelerating in an effort to travel across its greater distance and reach the wing's trailing edge at the same time as the particles on the underside. This acceleration reduces the air pressure above the curve and enables the heavier pressure below to lift the wing.

The kite also establishes two areas of differing pressure, but as said before, it does so in its own way. Held in place at the end of a line, it lies at an angle to the wind. Air particles are forced down its face. They "bunch" together at the base and so move slowly, thus increasing their pressure. Then they escape from under the base and flow up the back, racing now and reducing the pressure in their hurry to rejoin the particles coming over the top of the kite. With the air pressure increased at the lower front and decreased along the back, the kite rises or hovers aloft.

It is easy to see how the Bernoulli principle works with the kite of a single front-and-back surface. But what of the many-sided box kite? The principle remains the same. Now it simply operates with more than one surface.

Lift and Drag

While Bernoulli's principle enables the kite to get into the air, a number of other factors are also in play. They determine the manner in which the kite will fly and the heights to which it will ascend. Of these factors, the most fundamental are *lift* and *drag*. Lift refers to those forces that assist the Bernoulli principle in enabling the kite to defy the tug of gravity; they are, chiefly, the wind itself and the use that the kite's design makes of the wind. Drag, on the other hand, refers to all those features in the kite that resist the wind and exert a downward pull. They include the weight of the kite, its shape, and the surface of its covering.

In common with any object that flies, every kite has lift and drag. Because the kite is a thing of weight and dimensions, lift and drag cannot help but be present. In general, they influence flight in any one of three ways: If drag is at a maximum and lift at a minimum, the kite will tend to fly at a relatively low angle. If, however, the kite has much lift and little drag, it will be a highflier; heavy winds may give it a good buffeting up there, but, if it is strongly built and has sufficient drag, it will ride them successfully. Finally, if drag ever outweighs lift, the kite will be that greatest flying disappointment of all—the aerodyne that simply will not break free of the ground.

Talk about lift and drag often confuses and worries the beginning kite-maker-flier. But don't let it bother you. Time and a little experience will acquaint you with both factors. You'll soon be able to judge the effect that your kite's design, shape, and weight will have on them, and just as soon be able to make desired adjustments. Just let two points be your guide:

First, always do whatever you can to reduce drag by using

lightweight materials. Your materials, of course, will have to be of a weight and strength appropriate for the size and design of your kite. Obviously, a large kite needs heavier materials than does a small kite. And, obviously, the larger, heavier kite is not as likely to be batted about in a high wind as is its diminutive brother. Yet, always choose the lightest-weight materials appropriate for design and size. The strongly built lightweight kite is consistently the finest flier of all.

Second, even though always aiming to keep drag at a wise minimum, don't look on it as a villain. It helps to hold the kite steady and in place against the wind. As you'll soon see, the purpose of the kite tail is to supply needed stabilizing drag.

The other factors that join with lift and drag to influence the way a kite flies are several. They have to do with certain specifics of construction, and so we'll talk about them as we come to them, both in this chapter and in the ones that follow.

But now it's time to meet your kite.

Types of Kite

There are three basic types of kite: the *plane-surface* kite, the *bow* kite, and the *box* kite. Each takes its name from its appear-

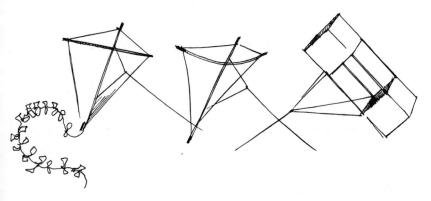

The basic types of kites—plane-surface, bow, and box

ance. Each will be given a separate chapter later in the book, followed by a folio of "unusual" kites. Though the "unusual" kites, which include many from the Orient, have shapes and contours all their own, you'll see that each is based on one or more of the basic three types.

The Plane-surface (Flat) Kite

The plane-surface kite is flat all across its face. Most often simply called the flat kite, it is the most basic of the three types. Yet it is quite as interesting as its two more sophisticated relatives, for, though pictured here in its conventional trapezoid form, it can be constructed in a variety of shapes. In Chapter 4, you'll find detailed instructions for shaping it into a hexagon, a diamond, a square, a star, and even a bird.

With its broad and flat face creating much drag, the kite ordinarily flies at a fairly low angle. It launches and flies nicely, but, thanks also to that flat face, it is easily buffeted by the wind and so always needs a tail for stability. Minus a tail, it will invariably treat you to a series of out-of-control aerobatics—complete with wild spins and loops—and likely conclude its performance with a nose dive into a tree or the ground.

Equipped with a tail, however, the flat kite is an easily handled, steady, and dependable performer.

The Bow Kite

The bow kite is simply a flat kite with its crosspiece arched back and held in a bow. It can have one or more bowed crosspieces and, not to be outdone by the flat kite, can assume a variety of shapes.

The bow gives the kite the *dihedral* (the rise along the crosspiece from its mid-points to its tips) of many airplane wings.

In its turn—for reasons that we'll see in Chapter 5—the dihedral gives the bow kite an advantage not enjoyed by its plane-surface relative. It enables the kite to fly with less drag and greater stability. Thanks to that stability, the bow kite can often be flown without a tail. Its stability also makes it an exceptionally good flier in high winds, winds that invariably expose every weakness to be found in the balance of a kite.

The Box Kite

In appearance, the box kite is the most distinctive of the three basic types. While the flat and the bow can be easily confused for each other at a distance, there is no mistaking the "flying crate," for it is the only one with three dimensions. It is also the youngest of the trio, having been invented in 1893 by Lawrence Hargrave of Australia. It has often been called one of the great modern innovations in kite design.

As you'll see in Chapter 6, the box kite can be built with a rigid frame (all members permanently locked in place) or a collapsible one for easy storage and transport. Its basic shapes are three—the square-cell, the oblong, and the triangle. These shapes, though interesting in themselves, can be modified into some of the most unusual-looking kites ever seen.

The box kite, by virtue of its several surfaces, exerts a great deal of drag. It is a very steady performer and can usually be flown without a tail.

Kite Size

All kites, from the most rudimentary of the basic to the most oddly shaped of the oriental models, can be built to practically any size desired. Miniature kites just a few inches long and wide have flown successfully, as have giants with spine lengths of ten feet or more.

But size must always be chosen with a practical eye. If you become too ambitious where it is concerned, it can easily damage the kite's flying potential.

For instance, if you begin scaling the kite too large, the weight of the materials will eventually interfere with lifting power. On the other hand, if you turn to smaller and smaller kites, they may at last prove too flimsy for the wind.

You're free, of course, to experiment with any size you wish. But it will be wise to save your experiments until you have become an accomplished craftsman with a solid understanding of design, materials, and flying conditions. In the meantime, stick with those kites recognized to be the most dependable fliers of all—those said to be of a conventional, or moderate, size. They are the ones that range from about two feet to a little more than three feet long.

The instructions for building the kites in this book will all be within this "conventional" range.

Parts of the Kite

Now that we've met the basic kites, let's take a moment to look at the parts that make each a whole. Some parts are so well known to everyone—and their functions so obvious—that we'll simply name them, just to get them on the record. Others will need a brief comment or two in addition to their names. As for the names themselves, some are technical and some semi-technical terms. All are said to belong to the "language of kiting."

THE SPINE:

The backbone of the kite, the spine is also known as a *longeron*, a term coming from the French and referring to any longitudinal stick in a kite. The longest sticks used in a box kite, whether they fly horizontally or longitudinally, are called spines.

THE SPAR:

The spar supports the wings of the kite. It is sometimes known as the *transverse piece* or the *crosspiece*.

THE FRAME:

The frame, which is just as often called the *framing string*, is a cord that extends from stick to stick and holds them in place, completing the kite skeleton. *Frame* also refers to the entire skeleton and to the covered kite.

THE BOWSTRING

THE COVER

THE FLYING LINE

THE BRIDLE:

An arrangement of one or more strings rising in front of the face, the bridle serves to hold the kite at a correct angle to the wind. Each string that extends out from the face to connect with the flying, or towing, line is called a *bridle leg*.

THE TOWING RING:

This is a metal or plastic ring that is sometimes used to connect a multi-legged bridle to the flying line.

THE TAIL

THE CELL:

A cell is any papered section of a box kite. Cells are also known as *units* and *sections*.

THE KEEL:

The keel is the spinal member to which the bridle is attached. Although illustrated here in the box kite, the term applies to all types of kites.

CROSSPIECES:

These are the smaller sticks in a box kite. They are used to give the kite shape and brace the skeleton.

These have been the basic terms that you'll need for a start. You'll come upon more in later chapters, but, because the "language of kiting" is not extensive, they will be few in number. Few though they may be, it will be wise for you to get them all straight in mind. With them, you'll find it easier to follow the directions for building the many kites described in the book. And, of course, if you've got your terminology down pat, you won't suffer the embarrassment of being confused or looking like a novice when you meet your first fellow enthusiast who really knows what he is talking about.

Kite Materials

As was said in Chapter 1, you can spend as little or as much money as you wish on kite-building and -flying. It's all up to you.

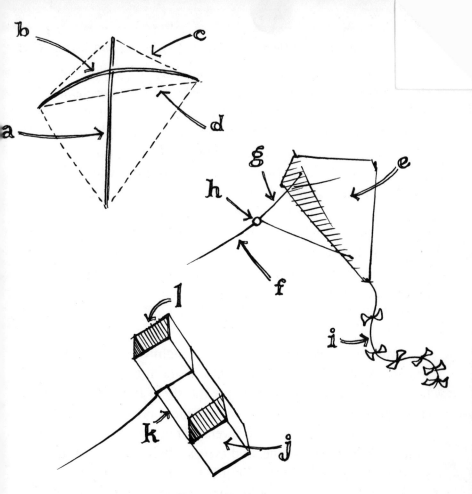

Parts of the kite

If you watch your pennies, kiting can be just about the most inexpensive hobby around. The supplies needed are few and simple. They are: sticks, string, and cover material.

We'll look at each in turn.

STICKS

You may make your own sticks or purchase them ready-made. Ready-made sticks come in several dimensions, and practically every hobby shop is sure to have an ample supply on hand.

Should you decide to make your own sticks, you'll find that

they can be cut from new or used lumber, strips of lath, or the sides of the wooden crates used to pack fruit and vegetables. Unfortunately, the crates—in the past, a rich source of kite sticks—are pretty much going out of style and are being replaced by cardboard boxes. Still, they haven't completely disappeared. A visit with your grocery store manager might prove worthwhile.

When first searching for stick material, don't make the mistake of thinking that the wood, to withstand the wind, must be hard and heavy. Such is not the case at all. Stick weight, naturally, will much depend on the size and design of your kite, but, remember, you're after the lightest frame possible. Too-heavy sticks unnecessarily weigh down the kite. Hard sticks have the nasty habit of not withstanding the wind at all—but of simply snapping in two.

And so, look for wood that is lightweight, flexible, and straight-grained. Lightweight wood will add minimum drag. Flexibility and a straight grain will give the sticks the "bend" and the strength necessary to meet the wind without breaking.

The woods best used are several. Topping the list are spruce, white pine, ponderosa pine, and cypress. Balsa wood may be used —but always with a caution: limit it to very small kites or to those models that use their sticks for shape rather than support (for instance, the Scott Sled described in Chapter 9). Otherwise, the soft balsa will not stand up to the strain.

Woods to be avoided are fir and redwood. Fir is both too hard and too heavy, while redwood is too brittle. Most cedars should be approached warily because they, too, are brittle, but there are some varieties that will prove satisfactory. If you have a cedar board on tap, you'd best show it to a knowledgeable friend to see if it is a suitable type.

Undoubtedly, bamboo is one of the finest of stick materials. Both strong and highly flexible, it can be used successfully in many conventional kites and is a "must" for the "spidery-framed" oriental kite.

You will need doweling for certain of your kites, among them the triangular box (Chapter 6). Doweling may be inexpensively purchased at all lumberyards and at most hardware stores and hobby shops. Usually found in three-foot lengths, it comes in a variety of diameters, from ⅛" up.

Nowadays, aluminum poles are manufactured for especially large kites. Also available are fiber-glass rods, which can be used in both conventional and large-sized kites. The poles and the rods, however, are on the expensive side, and there is no need to invest in them until, as a master kite maker, you come up with a design requiring them in place of wood.

Sticks may be cut from lumber, lath, or crate slats with a saw or a knife. In all cases, work slowly and carefully so that you don't damage the sticks or—more important—your fingers. When cutting a crate slat, mark the desired width and then, using a board or a yardstick as a guide, score either side of the slat, after which you can snap the stick free with your fingers. Bamboo sticks—which are easily obtained in great number from window shades (matchstick or slat), poles, or cane—can also be cut with a knife.

Once a stick is cut, it should be planed or sanded until it is smooth, balanced, and of the desired thickness. Incidentally, once you've cut a bamboo stick, you'll notice the characteristic "knuckles" at intervals along its length. They should be either hand- or power-sanded away.

The sticks in a kite of conventional size usually measure from ⅛" to ⅜" thick and from ¼" to ⅛" wide. Using these dimensions as a rule-of-thumb standard, you can then reduce or increase stick width and thickness according to the actual size of your kite. Aside from the need to use the lightest-weight materials feasible, there are no really hard-and-fast rules governing exact stick dimensions for a given kite size. In the directions for constructing the kites in this book, recommended stick dimensions will be given to get you started. Once you're on your own, experience and a little common sense will point the way to the stick dimensions needed for each kite that you build.

STRING

String is put to four uses in the kite. It serves as framing material, bridling material, flying line, and tail line.

Framing Material: Ordinary string, tough and thin, will prove perfectly satisfactory for most kites. Miniatures will probably need a strong thread, and intricately shaped oriental kites will assuredly require reed-thin bamboo strips. Very large kites may call for nylon cord or even a slender clothesline.

Bridling Material: Ordinary string, twine, or a thin cord will do nicely for practically all bridles. For a reason you'll see in a moment, the bridle material should equal the strength of the flying line.

Flying Line: Here the choices are many. String, hemp twine, cotton or linen cord, seine cord, nylon or dacron (twisted or braided), monofilament nylon, fishing line, and thread (button or regular) —all will serve you well, with your choice, naturally, depending on the weight and size of your kite. Of the lot, nylon fishing line is thought by many kite makers to be the best all-round performer.

Always, as with your other materials, choose the lightest-weight line possible for the job. You want your kite to fly high, but the line, having weight and dimension, will always tend to pull it down. Even a very lightweight line, when enough of it is unreeled, exerts a significant downward pull. The wind then does its bit by blowing against the line and shaping it into an arc that drops the kite still lower. With a too-heavy line, the whole problem can quickly become a genuine headache.

To select the right minimum weight, you'll need to estimate the expected pull of the kite against the line. Every line has its breaking, or test, strength, which is measured in pounds. Should the tug of the kite ever exceed that strength, you'll be faced with a new problem. The line will divide and you'll have to stand there and watch the result of all your work go drifting into the sunset. But how do you compute the test strength needed for a given pull?

Thanks to Wyatt Brummitt, the author of *Kites*, the job is made easy by a simple formula. Just estimate the frontal surface of the kite in square feet and then multiply that figure by three. If your kite has a facial surface of nine square feet $(3' \times 3')$, you'll know that you need a line with a test strength of twenty-seven pounds. Say that your kite is six feet square $(3' \times 2')$; you'll want an eighteen-pound line.

So that test strengths match, it will be wise to make the bridle of lengths cut from the flying line.

Flying line, packaged in varying lengths and marked with its test strength, can be purchased at hardware stores and hobby shops. But, if you're watching your pennies, why don't you scout the house to see what's lying around? Forgotten fishing line will prove a real "find" for many a kite. Cord or twine with a test strength of twenty-five pounds can be safely used with conventional-sized and somewhat larger kites in most all wind conditions. Ten-pound cord is fine for small kites, and ordinary string will usually handle them well at heights up to around a hundred yards. A strong button thread will fly very small kites successfully. But think twice about tying ordinary string to a three-footer. It isn't likely to stand the strain.

Just one word of Caution (with a capital C!) about the flying line. Sooner or later, some fellow enthusiast is going to tell you that wire is the finest line of all and that it is used when meteorologists send kites aloft for weather observations. He'll be right on both counts, but don't let him talk you into being another Benjamin Franklin. Wire line is dangerous. There is always the hazard of lightning discharge or contact with overhead electric lines. Need more be said?

The Tail: Ordinary string, a lightweight cord or twine, or even thread (for the very small kite) are all suitable for use. Handsome, decorative tails for oriental kites are to be had simply by cutting streamers from rolls of narrow crepe paper. We'll talk more at length about tails in the next chapter.

COVER

A few minutes spent poking about the house will usually net you all the cover material necessary for your first building efforts. What you're after is a paper or a cloth light enough for the frame, airtight enough to ride the wind, and strong enough to resist tearing. Such covering is to be found everywhere.

Large kites, obviously, leave greater areas of unsupported material vulnerable to the wind, and so require a stronger cover. Ordinary tissue paper is hardy enough for flat kites up to three feet, but butcher paper or brown wrapping paper is safer for flats of somewhat larger dimensions. Large flats and bows of all sizes are best covered with a lightweight cloth or plastic, though paper will work well in bows up to slightly larger-than-average sizes.

Quite as important as strength is airtightness. To ride the wind successfully, the cover should allow as little air as possible to pass through it. Most papers are pretty airtight, but some cloths can give you trouble. In your search through the house, side-step such materials as cheesecloth; they're far too porous. On the other hand, cotton and rayon are to be welcomed; discarded curtains often yield fine cover material. And, should you ever come across a piece of high grade silk that no one wants, you've struck a kite maker's "gold mine." Expensive, durable, and highly airtight, it makes an excellent cover. It is, however, a difficult cloth to handle, so work with it carefully.

As you move to expert status, you'll probably want to experiment with materials other than those found around the house. Strong grades of tissue and crepe paper may be purchased, as can fine sailcloths and various plastics. Among the plastics are polyethylene and such brand-name synthetics as Mylar and Tyvek, both manufactured by the Du Pont company. Polyethylene is durable and inexpensive; in very thin sheets, it may tend to stretch or tear, but it can be easily tightened or repaired with tape. Both Mylar and Tyvek are exceptionally strong, with the latter being almost impossible to tear.

All right. You've met the kite, its various parts, and the materials of which it's made. Now let's get to your worktable. Let's get ready to build.

3

BUILDING YOUR KITE

In this chapter, we'll be talking about those basic construction techniques needed to launch you safely as a kite maker. Though some may be used with kites of an advanced and radical design, most are intended for the models that practically every builder first tries—the flats and bows. Certain tips for the construction of the box kite will be saved until later.

We'll begin by taking a brief look at the working equipment you should have for a start.

Working Equipment

Your working equipment can be summed up with the same word used to describe the kite's materials: simple. All that you need have at hand are:

1. A knife
2. A ruler (18″ is a practical length) or a yardstick
3. A small, thin-bladed hand saw
4. Scissors
5. A file or a few pieces of fine- to medium-grain sandpaper

6. A roll of transparent or cloth tape
7. A box of the cloth rings used to reinforce the holes in loose-leaf paper
8. A few rubber bands
9. Some modelmaker's glue and white glue (or rubber cement)
10. A right-angle rule or—don't laugh—a sheet from the classified section of the newspaper.

For the most part, nothing needs be said about the equipment. But a few of the items deserve a comment or two. The knife, of course, should be sharp, and may be either a small kitchen or pocket knife (stay away from butcher knives and the like—they're unwieldy and dangerous). Recommended is the Exacto knife; if you don't already own one, it's a purchase worth thinking about. The cloth reinforcing rings may puzzle you; they're used to strengthen the holes that must be made in the paper for certain bridles. And what on earth is the sheet from the newspaper's classified section good for?

For as long as you're building kites, you'll be crossing sticks at right angles. If you're without a right-angle rule, the news sheet will serve in its place. Just tape the sheet to your work surface and draw a heavy pencil or crayon line across it, using one of the horizontal lines separating the ads as a guide. Then intersect it with a heavy line down the page, this time following one of the vertical lines dividing the columns. When you align your sticks at the intersection, they'll be at perfect right angles. Okay?

Now for the basic construction tips:

Slits, Notches, and Grooves

When you are building the flat or bow kite your first job will be to prepare the stick ends so that the framing string can be at-

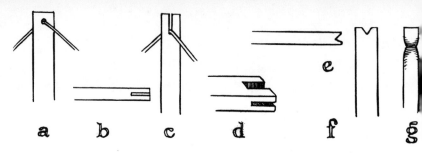

Holes, single slits, double slits, and notches

tached securely to them. The simplest way to prepare the stick ends is to drill a small hole through each (a) and pass the framing string through each hole as it circles the skeleton. The more advanced method of preparation is to dress the stick ends with slits or notches.

As you can see, there are several slits and notches. Each kite maker has his preference. Time and experience will point out your own favorites.

Single slits can be made in either of two ways—by cutting horizontally into the thickness of the stick (b) or perpendicularly along its width (c). In either case, they should run to about ¼″ deep. They may be cut with a thin-bladed hand saw or a knife, with some builders preferring to "etch" them out by placing a heated wire against the wood. Should you decide on a hand saw, you will be wise to place each stick in a vise or otherwise lock it in place so that it doesn't "shudder" with every blade stroke and finally break.

The single slit may be used in either the flat or the bow kite, with the single cut holding both the framing string and the bowstring in the latter. If you wish, you may fashion double slits for the bow kite (d). Now the horizontal cut takes the framing string, and the perpendicular cut the bowstring. Again, the cuts should be about ¼″ deep.

Many kite makers like to notch rather than slit the stick ends. Notches can be set into the thickness (e) or the width (f). Some builders who prefer the notch argue that it facilitates kite repair. The sticks in most flat and bow kites can be removed for repair or

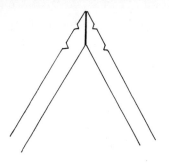

Additional use of the notch

replacement without disturbing the cover, and the angled opening in the notch seems to make the freeing of the string from the stick a bit easier.

Kites with dowel spars often need a groove (g) to hold the framing string or the bowstring in place. The groove circles the spar and should be cut about ⅛" deep. If used in conjunction with slits or notches, it should be inscribed just beyond their inner terminals.

Now let's go back to the notch for a moment. It serves an additional purpose in the kite.

Notches are needed when two sticks join in an arrow point. Here, the notches are made in the outer edges of each stick, near the tip of the point at its base. They hold in place the thread or string used to bind the join.

Lashing

It goes without saying that the sticks in a kite need to be lashed together at the points where they cross each other. You may lash the sticks with tape or line. Either method works well. Again, you're free to choose your favorite.

When the first of the methods is used, the sticks should be lashed with adhesive tape. Using two short strips the width of the sticks, lap them over the spar, as illustrated, and then wrap each diagonally around the sticks. Don't completely wrap off one entire

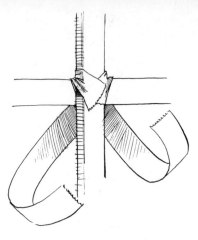

Lashing with tape

strip before turning to the other. You'll get a better job by alternating between the strips as you go, giving one a turn or two, and then switching to the other.

Tape can be used to lash three and four sticks. The process of wrapping is essentially the same as in the diagram.

Tape, especially when it is of the "super-sticky" variety, serves as a quite secure lashing. It is advised for the smaller kite, but it can pose a problem in larger models. It can result in a bulky lashing, and so, while many fine builders use it, most kite makers prefer a line lashing.

Should you elect to go along with the majority, you'll end up with a very secure lashing if you follow the steps in the next illustration. Be sure to complete your work with a square knot. It protects against the string loosening.

Ordinary string or a strong cotton or linen thread may be used as line lashings in conventional-sized kites. Larger kites may need a thin cord, while thread is the best bet for smaller kites.

For a truly strong join the sticks should be prepared for the lashing. It is wise to sand them at the join points so that they adhere better to each other. It is also wise to use a coating of model-maker's glue on their outside faces; the glue will soak up through the string, "grabbing" it and locking it into place as you work. Fi-

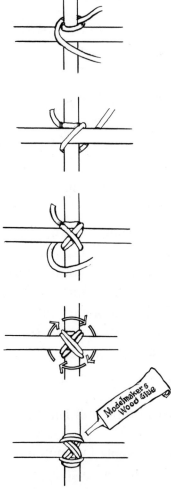

Steps in line lashing

nally, if you wish, you may coat the finished lashing with waterproof cement or glue to reinforce it and seal down the knot and string ends.

When joining exceptionally large sticks, you may need to crosscut them at their intersection to help keep them locked together. But *never use the crosscut* unless absolutely necessary. It weakens the sticks too much at the very point where the kite takes its greatest strain. And crosscut sparingly with even very large sticks, taking care to keep the cuts as shallow as possible.

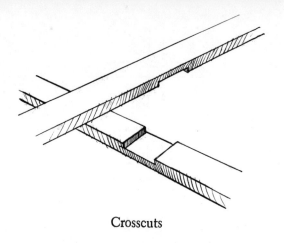

Crosscuts

A line lashing is also known as a mechanical join. Some commercially made kites have mechanical joins made of metal staples so that the sticks can be rotated and thus closed into a single unit for easy packaging. Some kite makers like this system and so fashion their own staples. And, if you're willing to spend the money, you can buy plastic joins—not only for the spar and spine intersection, but for the base and top of the kite as well.

Framing and Binding

The kite is framed simply by running a string from stick to stick, inserting it in the slits or notches as you go along, and then knotting it off when you return to your starting point. The string should be drawn taut between sticks, but should not be pulled so tight that it warps the sticks.

You may begin framing from either the top or the bottom of the kite. Some kite makers feel that it is wise to frame from the bottom, especially when working with a model such as the diamond, which you'll meet in Chapter 4. They feel that a kite such as this, having a somewhat narrow face, is given a degree more stability when the weight of the framing string knot is at the bottom. Others like to frame from the base so that they can tie the tail line to the free ends of the framing string.

Whichever way you choose to frame, you'll want to keep the framing string from slipping while you work. This may be done by looping it around the first of the slits and loosely knotting it. Otherwise, you may double knot the string about six inches or so from its end. When pulled against the slit, the knot will keep the string from slipping further.

The strain of flight or the pressure of the framing string may prove too much for the wood around a slit or notch. Each slit and notch should be reinforced with a binding of string or thread.

You're free to bind the stick in one operation, but for safety's sake, you really should divide the job into two steps, first doing a half-bind at the inner terminal of the slit before inserting the framing string, and then finishing off the binding after the frame is complete. There's nothing quite so frustrating as seeing the framing string snap off one side of an unbound slit. It can—and does—happen from time to time as the string is being drawn to the next stick.

And so the two-step bind is always advised. For the first step, give the string three or four turns around the inner terminal of the slit, tie it off with a square knot, and let the string ends dangle. Later, when the job needs to be completed, extend string end a

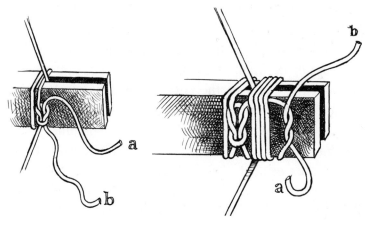

Two-step binding

along the stick as shown, and wrap end b around the slit three or four times, carrying it in front of the framing string and over the top of a. Finish off your work with a square knot.

Ordinary string or a strong thread will serve well for bindings. It's a good idea to reinforce all bindings and seal in the string ends with a coating of glue or waterproof cement, just as you do with the lashings.

Covering

Once the framing is complete, the kite is ready for its cover. The cover is made and attached in three steps. Let's try them with a paper cover.

First, spread out and smooth down a cover sheet substantially larger than the kite. Place the frame on it to serve as a guide and outline the kite on the sheet, making the outline at least ¾" to 1" oversize.

Next, cut out the cover and trim it at all stick ends, as illustrated. The trimming converts the oversize into flaps that are to be folded back over the framing string. Don't be afraid to trim the paper at the distance indicated from the stick ends. With the paper well clear of the ends, you'll be better able to remove the sticks for later repair or replacement without disturbing the cover.

Finally, again place the frame on the sheet. After making sure that all legs of the framing string are parallel to and an equal distance from the edges of the cover, fold the flaps back over the strings and glue down. Spread the glue evenly and coat the string with it so that string and paper become a single unit.

White glue attaches the paper cover efficiently and smoothly, as does rubber cement. Avoid modelmaker's glue, for it's apt to cause the paper to wrinkle. If you're a dedicated "do-it-yourself" builder, you can make your own paste by mixing flour and water into a semi-liquid state. Cook your recipe to a boil. It will then dry almost clear when applied.

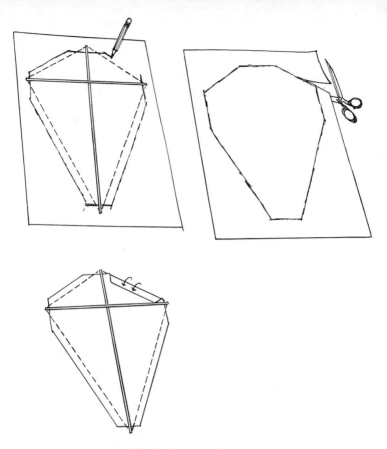

Steps in covering

Should you turn to a cover material other than paper, you'll have to abandon the glue and rubber cement. Practically all plastics must be held in place with tape. Either cloth or cellulose tape will fill the bill; Mystik tape, because it is both inexpensive and lightweight, is a good choice. Cloth covers should be sewn to the framing string, although cotton and silk will take a fabric glue.

Incidentally, the method for attaching a sewn cloth cover differs radically from that for a paper cover. Since it's rather an advanced method, we need not go into it just yet. We'll save it for Chapter 6, when you begin to build the bow kite.

Once the paper cover is in place, it may be a bit wrinkled. If so, you can tighten it by spraying it with water; if yours is a painted cover, spray the kite on the back so that you won't damage the paint. But, remember, just *spray*—preferably with an atomizer. Don't soak the kite in the sink. You'll draw the paper too tight. Once sprayed, place the kite in a shaded, well-ventilated place where it will dry evenly.

One last point: If you're going to paint your cover, do so before attaching it to the frame. You'll get a neater job and will run less risk of damaging the paper.

Cover Decoration

Now that we've mentioned it, let's talk for a moment about cover decoration.

Here, you can let your imagination be your guide. Your kite cover may be decorated in any way that pleases you—with names, faces, cartoon characters, animals, polka dots, stars, abstract designs, stripes, or masses of dots sprinkled on with a paint brush. The choice of what is done is entirely up to you and your artistic sense. In fact, in allowing your imagination to be your guide, you can just about let it "run away with you."

Although you're free to select whatever decoration you wish, you should follow three common-sense rules. First, while giving your imagination full rein, do not let it so carry you away that the decoration weakens the kite or interferes with its flying ability. For instance, avoid brushing on thick layers of paint; they can weigh the kite down unnecessarily and are apt after a time to split and tear the cover material. Such decorations as flags and pennants may be flown from the kite. Make sure, however, that they are placed at points that will not throw the kite out of balance.

Second, always remember that your decoration is to be viewed from a distance. Avoid combining colors that tend to merge as the kite rides away from the eye. For instance, areas of blue and orange might provide a startling contrast while you're painting them onto the cover. But, once in the air, they will merge into a gray. To avoid a loss of contrast, run bands of a striking dark color between the two or separate them with areas of a darker or lighter hue.

Finally, should you decide to try an abstract design, keep it on the simple side, separating its various colors and areas. As with colors, an intricate design up close may look as if it belongs in an art gallery. But, at a distance, it will lose its detail.

The agents used for kite decoration are many. Poster paints, acrylic paints, water-color paints, inks, vegetable dyes, and crayons —all have been used successfully, as have such methods as batiking, silk-screening, block-printing, and stenciling. Interesting decorations are to be had by cementing variously colored and oddly shaped pieces of tissue paper to the cover or, if the skeleton permits, by building a cover of two or three different colored tissues.

For many a kite man, cover decoration is quite as important as any other aspect of construction. It is his "finishing touch"—the touch that gives his kite its individuality and rounds out its beauty.

The Bridle

The bridle is a cord, or a series of cords, that links the kite to the flying line. It is your most important operational control, for when properly set its cords hold the kite at a correct angle to the breeze and make efficient flight possible. Proper setting, however, depends much on the winds of the day, and so the cords should be arranged in a way that makes them easily adjustable. In a few moments, then, you can have the kite set at the exact angle needed for best performance.

There are several types of bridles. Each is named for the number of cord lengths—legs—in it. Here are the types most frequently used. Let's talk about each for a moment.

THE ONE-LEG BRIDLE

The one-leg bridle is the simplest of the lot and consists of just the flying line. The line passes through one hole punched in the cover at the spine-spar intersection, loops around the inter-

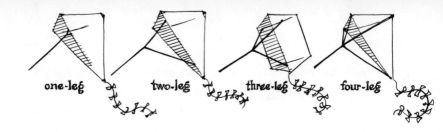

Types of bridles

section, comes back out an adjoining hole, and is securely tied off a few inches out from the kite face. The one-leg bridle works quite well for some kites, but most models need two or more legs for stability.

Incidentally, it's at this point that you'll use those cloth reinforcing rings in your list of work items for the first time. Whenever you punch a hole in the cover, be sure to circle it with a ring to prevent future tearing. If you have no rings handy, small pieces of transparent tape will do in their place.

THE TWO-LEG BRIDLE

The two-leg bridle is made by extending a string from the top of the kite to the bottom and then joining it to the flying line in any of three ways.

First, you may knot the flying line directly to the bridle; in this case, you'd best secure the tie-point with transparent tape to keep the line from slipping along the bridle and changing the angle of flight. Second, a loop knot can be made in the completed bridle and the line then passed through it. Or, as you are building the bridle, you may loop it through a towing ring at the appropriate point on the kite face; if the loop is made as illustrated, you'll have no trouble moving the ring up or down to its final location.

Metal washers or the strong plastic rings found in drapery shops make fine towing rings. Some kite makers loop several rings into the bridle in the approximate area of the line join. They then

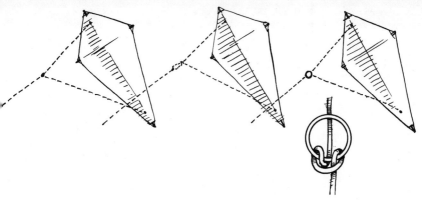

Two-leg bridle tie-offs

use the one that proves to give the best flight angle on a given day. Often, they secure a swivel fastener to the end of the flying line so that they can switch from ring to ring without the bother of untying the line.

THE THREE-LEG BRIDLE

This bridle is limited principally to kites of a special design, such as the Baden-Powell levitor. For attachment to the flying line, the leg ends may be tied to a towing ring or they may all be gathered together and knotted into a loop.

THE FOUR-LEG BRIDLE

Here we have lines coming from the top and bottom of the spine, and from either end of the spar. They form an especially stabilizing pattern that makes the four-legger one of the most popular of bridles. Lashed as they are to all stick ends, they distribute the wind evenly over the facial surface and thus hold the kite very steadily into the wind.

The flying line attachment for the four-leg bridle is the same as for the three-legger. The cord ends may be tied to a towing ring or gathered together and knotted in a loop.

You may also make the bridle with just two cords, running

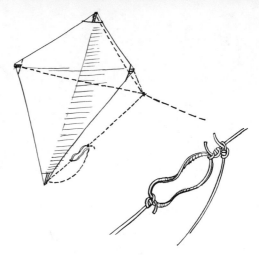

Self-adjusting bridle

one the length of the spine, and the other across the spar. The
flying line can then be tied directly to the intersection. Again, it's
wise to secure the knot with a piece of tape so that the line will not
slip.

ANGLE OF SETTING

Now let's talk about properly setting the legs so that they give
the best angle of flight.

They should always be set so that the kite "leans" into the
wind and establishes the opposing areas of air pressure needed for
lift. The lean, however, must be just right. If the setting is too low
the kite will stand somewhat straight, take the wind head-on, and
dart from side to side or refuse to lift. If the setting is too high, the
kite will "flatten" out and lose the increased air pressure along it
lower face. The result: You'll have a kite that dips, flutters, or sim
ply thrashes about helplessly.

You'll get a good beginning "lean" by first joining the leg
and flying line at a point about one-third the way down the face—
at about the spine-spar join in many kites. That point of attach
ment might prove perfectly satisfactory. Your first flight of the day
will tell. Adjustments are made by moving the bridle up or down
the flying line or by shortening or lengthening various of the cords

You should adjust the bridle a bit at a time—actually, about an inch at a time—so that you don't inadvertently go past the correct setting. All this may seem a bother at first, but you'll soon find the adjustments easy to make, and of course, your growing experience should eventually reduce them to a minimum.

A few tips will help you along the way to finding the correct lean. The flat kite generally flies best at a 45° angle, while bows and boxes do best at a slightly flatter incline. The bridle should always be set at the highest tow point possible before fluttering occurs; the point must be particularly high when the wind is heavy, for then the kite needs to fly at a flatter angle than usual. It's a good idea to tie the bridle legs to the kite with a clove hitch; the loop at the flying line connection is best made with the bowknot or the clove hitch. These knots are easily untied and will speed the work of adjustment. Any solid knot at the towing ring will do well; it can be quickly cut away with a knife.

The bridle legs should meet the flying line a distance out from the cover face so that the kite will have some flexibility of movement when flying. The distance varies among kites. In general, it should not be great enough to enable the legs, when pulled, to reach the end of the spar. As with "lean," proper bridle distance will usually need to be determined by a few moments of trial-and-error experimentation.

These bridles are all basic types and, of course, must be adjusted by hand. A more advanced type is the elastic bridle, which is able to adjust itself to wind changes while the kite is aloft. The self-adjustment is made possible by a rubber band attached to the lower bridle leg.

The Tail

As you know, the tail is a "must" for all flat kites and some bows. Its job is to provide stability, a job that it does in two ways.

First, it flows out behind the kite parallel to the wind and

Clove hitch in bow

creates a drag that faces the kite into the wind—just as a rudder keeps a ship on course. Second, it counteracts the sudden twists and turns to which every kite, especially the flat, is vulnerable. These twists and turns, so often caused by the wind gusting, trigger a series of wavelike motions that travel down the kite and into the tail. The tail begins to snake from side to side, steadies the kite, and brings it back on course.

The tail also adds a bit of stabilizing weight to the kite. But weight, as usual, should be kept at a minimum, with your attention being given more to length. Correct length is all-important. If too short, the tail will not be able to snake and control those twists and turns. If too long (or too heavy), it will cause the kite to "wag" from side to side, an action that is very destabilizing. But at the right length, the tail line will flow out behind the kite in a gentle dance and do all that it is supposed to do.

But what is the right length? Lengths will be recommended for the kites met throughout this book. To figure the length for models of your own, it's a good idea to start with a tail line approximately four times as long as the kite is diagonal. Once the kite is aloft, its design and the strength of the wind will tell you how close on the mark you are. A little experimentation will then do the rest. Always take a knife and additional tail materials along on your flights. They'll be needed more times than not.

Ordinary string will prove a fine tail line for most kites. It should be given drag by placing paper, plastic, or lightweight cloth bows at intervals along its length. Cut the bows 2″×6″ and space

them from 6" to 1' apart (some kite makers recommend 4" to 6").
Do not knot the bows around the line, but rather, tie the line to
the bows, doing so with the clove hitch, as illustrated. Otherwise
they'll insist on sliding down the line.

The tail can be adjusted for various winds by shortening or
lengthening the line, by moving the bows closer together or farther apart, or by changing their number. Strong winds will require
a tail longer than usual. In fact, as some kite makers say, the
stronger the wind, the longer the tail must be.

Crepe streamers may be used as tail lines. They are particularly appropriate for oriental kites, and they should be used at all
times on any kite—such as the eight-point star (Chapter 4)—that
requires more than one tail line. When two or more string lines are
flown from the kite they have the bad habit of tangling together.

At times, especially when flying a very wide kite or a kite with
a broad top, you may need to add much wind drag to the tail before stability is achieved. This extra drag can be had with the
windcup, or drogue.

Windcups can be easily made from cardboard or stiff paper.
Their sizes will vary according to the size of the kite. For the kite
of average dimensions, try making them each about 5" deep, 3" in

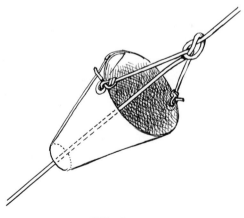

Windcup

diameter at the top, and 1″ in diameter at the bottom. The cups fly with their wide openings into the wind and with the tail line threaded through circular holes 1″ wide in their bottoms.

The cups provide stability by catching the air and constricting it before allowing it to escape through the holes in their bottoms. They should be attached at one-foot intervals along the tail line. If you're not in the mood to fashion your own cups, you might find that a few paper drinking cups will serve you well.

And that's it. With the techniques explained in this chapter, you're ready to begin building.

4

THE FLAT KITE

Of the three basic types of kite, the simplest to build is the plane-surface, or flat, kite.

As a beginning builder, you'll find it the ideal kite on which to develop your construction skills. You'll get ample practice at tying, framing, and covering, but you'll be working on just one flat surface all the while. There will be no need to worry about the precise bracings that go into the box kite, and no need even to think about the dihedral of the bow kite. And, although you'll never want to build in careless haste, you won't have to wait for days before sending your "masterpiece" aloft to check your workmanship. Most flat kites can be constructed in an hour or so.

But, simple though it may be to put together, the flat kite won't bore you. It offers a variety of interesting challenges, even for the experienced builder.

For instance, it can be built with from two to four sticks and, as was said earlier, can be fashioned in a number of shapes, several of which can be modified into still other shapes. It sails along happily at any practical size, either large or small. And the expanse of its face presents endless design possibilities. You can literally let your imagination and your paint brush "run away with themselves."

And so you're in for an interesting time with the following instructions. With them, you'll be able to build eleven flat kites—six of which are basic models—each with a shape quite its own, while the remaining five are simple but unusual variations of certain of the basic models. The measurements given throughout will be those for kites of a conventional size. If you wish to build to a larger or smaller scale, all that you need do is keep the proportions approximately the same and make certain that the materials are of a strength appropriate for the frame.

Using the construction tips given in Chapter 3, we'll first build two simple kites of two sticks each. From there, we'll advance to models needing three sticks and then end with a "four-sticker."

Ready? Here we go.

The Two-stick Kite

The two-stick flat kite, or "two-sticker" as it is commonly called, is the easiest of all kites to build. Forming a trapezoid, it is also the most traditional looking of kites, the one said to be the most "kite-shaped." We'll look first at the materials needed and then construct it in three steps—(1) frame, (2) cover, and (3) bridle and tail.

MATERIALS

1. One flat spine, $\frac{1}{8}'' \times \frac{3}{8}'' \times 36''$
2. One flat spar, $\frac{1}{8}'' \times \frac{3}{8}'' \times 30''$
3. Cover sheet, $36'' \times 40''$
4. String and working equipment

FRAME

1. Start by slitting the ends of each stick and doing a half-bind at the inner terminal of each slit.

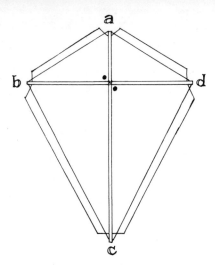

Two-stick Kite

2. Next, place the exact mid-point of the spar at right angles to the spine 8″ below the top of the spine. Lash the two pieces together with string and tie off. Remember, it's a good idea to coat the wrapping with waterproof cement or glue.

3. Now insert the framing string in slit a and then run it around the kite, inserting it into the other slits as you go, and returning at last to tie off at slit a. A reminder: Stretch the string taut, but do not pull it so tight that it warps the sticks.

4. Once the framing string is in place and tied off, check the spar to see if you disturbed its right-angle join with the spine as you worked. If so, adjust the spar accordingly. Finally, complete the bindings at each slit. Don't forget to coat the bindings.

COVER

1. Spread out the cover sheet, smoothing it down all over, and position the kite frame on it. Draw an outline of the kite on the cover, giving it the ¾″ to 1″ overlap suggested in Chapter 3. When you cut out the cover check the illustration and, as indicated, trim the overlap into tabs by notching it at the points where it meets the stick ends.

2. Again, place the frame on the cover, this time making cer-

tain that the spar is beneath the spine. (When flown, a kite will have greater strength if the spar is to the front of the spine.) Fold the tabs over the framing string and cement them into place.

> TIP: While outlining the cover or gluing down the tabs, you may need to keep the frame from shifting. If so, you may fasten the sticks to the cover with three or four small pieces of transparent tape. Keep the pieces small, though, and press them just lightly into place so that they won't tear the cover material when they are finally removed.

BRIDLE AND TAIL

1. Though the kite may be flown with a one- or two-leg bridle, many kite makers feel that it performs best with the four-legger. Make the bridle of your choice according to the instructions in Chapter 3. If you decide on the two- or four-legger, leave enough play in the legs so that when pulled they ride out about 6″ to 8″ in front of the spar-spine join. Tie the flying line to the bridle at this point.

2. Attach the tail to the base of the spine, trying about eight feet of line with paper, plastic, or lightweight cloth bows spaced along it at the intervals suggested in Chapter 3. But be sure to take along a pocket knife and extra line on your test flights. The wind will tell you whether the line needs to be shortened or lengthened.

And that's all there is to it. Shall we try another model?

The Arch-top Kite

The arch-top is a variation of the trapezoid kite. It was born in Malaya, came to Europe in the seventeenth century, and later won such popularity in England that many kite makers now refer

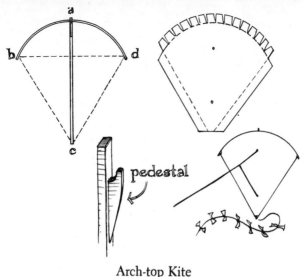

Arch-top Kite

to it as the "English arch-top." It is the kite that George Pocock used to pull his carriage along at those speeds of around twenty miles an hour.

MATERIALS

1. One flat spine, $\frac{1}{8}'' \times \frac{1}{4}'' \times 36''$
2. One spar, flexible dowel, $\frac{3}{16}'' \times 36''$
3. One pedestal stick, $\frac{1}{4}'' \times \frac{1}{4}'' \times 1\frac{1}{2}''$
4. Cover sheet, $36'' \times 40''$
5. String and working equipment

FRAME

1. Slit and half-bind the spine at end c and the spar at either tip. Then, just beyond the inner terminals of the spar slits, circle the dowel with grooves, making them deep enough to hold two or three turns of a string, but not so deep as to weaken the wood. The top of the spine does not need a slit.

2. Now fashion the pedestal to the shape shown in the illustration and glue it into position about $\frac{1}{2}''$ down from the top of

the kite. A tightly wound rubber band will hold the pedestal in place while the glue is drying.

3. At this point, you're in for your first experience at bowing a stick. Gently arch the spar into a bow by drawing a string between slits b and d. The spar should be bowed until the distance between its tips measures 31" to 32". Finish binding the slits and —a reminder—coat the binds with cement or glue.

> TIP: The spar, flexible to begin with, should bend easily. If it resists a bit, however, run it under hot water for a few moments to soften it and make it more "bendable."

4. Seat the spar on the pedestal and ease it down into place. Be sure that the spar is seated at its exact mid-point and that its tips are level with each other. Lash both the spar and the pedestal to the spine, finishing off the wrap with a cement or glue coating. Finally, tie the bowstring to the spine.

5. Now you'll need to measure the distance from stick end b to c to d, after which a piece of string should be cut at least 8" longer than that distance. Insert the mid-point of the string into c, and then run one string end to groove b, the other to groove d. Wrap each string end into place with two or three turns, tie off, and coat the wrapping. You'd best check to see if you pushed the spar tips out of alignment during framing. If so, correct the alignment. Complete your work by finishing and coating the binding at slit c.

> TIP: Until you get the hang of it, you will undoubtedly have some trouble lashing the framing string to the spar without getting the tips far out of alignment. Once the string is in slit c, you can make life easier for yourself by anchoring the sticks to your worktable with strips of transparent tape before proceeding. Do not, however, set the tape too close to the spar tips. Leave a little space so that the tips will remain flexible and be in no danger of snapping off.

COVER

1. Place the frame on the cover and draw an outline of the kite on the cover, giving it the recommended ¾″ to 1″ overlap. Cut out the cover and notch the overlap at the stick ends. Then, as shown in the illustration, divide the overlap into a series of tabs along the spar so that they will fold neatly over the arch. Each tab should be about 2″ to 3″ wide.

2. Align the frame once more on the cover. Cement the overlap over the spar and framing strings. It's a good idea to cement along the arch first and then along each string.

BRIDLE AND TAIL

1. The arch-top flies well with either a two- or four-leg bridle. If you choose the latter, rig it just as you did for the two-sticker. For the two-legger, carefully punch two holes in the cover directly in front of the spine—one 6″ from the top of the kite, the other 9″ from the bottom. Remember to strengthen each with a reinforcing ring for loose-leaf paper, and then extend the bridle string from one hole to the other. Leave enough play in the string for a space of 6″ to 8″ between the bridle and the kite face at a point slightly above the intersection of the spine and bowstring.

2. Just as you did with the two-sticker, fasten an eight-foot tail line to the base of the kite. As before, space paper, plastic, or lightweight cloth bows along its length. And, as before, take along a knife and some extra string on your test flight.

The Diamond Kite

Now, still using just two sticks, let's try for yet another shape —this time a diamond.

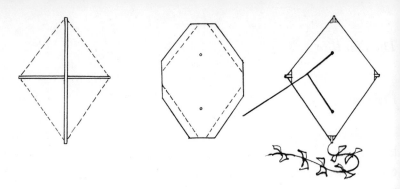

Diamond Kite

MATERIALS

1. One flat spine, $\frac{1}{8}'' \times \frac{3}{8}'' \times 36''$
2. One flat spar, $\frac{1}{8}'' \times \frac{3}{8}'' \times 25''$
3. Cover sheet, $30'' \times 40''$
4. String and working equipment

FRAME

1. Slit and half-bind all stick ends.

2. Placing them at right angles, cross the spar and spine at their exact mid-points and lash them together.

3. Frame the kite with string. Check the spar to see that it is still perfectly horizontal to the spine and, if necessary, adjust it accordingly. All binds should then be finished off.

COVER

1. Using the frame as a guide, outline and then cut out the cover, leaving the customary overlap. As shown in the illustration, the cover points need to be cut away—"stubbed"—at all stick ends.

2. Cement the overlap over the framing strings. It is best to cement the top half of the cover into place and then concentrate on the bottom half.

BRIDLE AND TAIL

1. Either a four- or a two-leg bridle will do nicely for the diamond. The first is built just as it was for the two-sticker, the second just as it was for the arch-top. This time, if you choose the two-leg bridle, punch the cover holes 8″ from the top and bottom of the spine. Don't forget to strengthen them with reinforcing rings.

2. Once again, an eight-foot tail line, festooned with bows along its length, is advised for a start.

And now we come to the first of our variations:

A Variation: *The Square Kite*

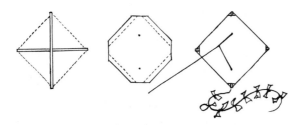

Square Kite

Once you've built the diamond kite, you can easily fashion a different-shaped model by using two sticks of the same length. Just follow the instructions for the diamond kite, and you'll soon be flying its brother—the square kite. Why don't you try sticks 24″ or 25″ long? As illustrated, holes for a two-leg bridle should be punched 5″ from the top and bottom of the spine. Attach an eight-foot tail line.

The Three-stick Kite

Thus far we've worked with just two sticks. Now let's add a third to the list. It will give us the basic "three-sticker," a hexagon shaped kite that flies easily and presents an especially broad sur face for imaginative design.

MATERIALS

1. Two flat spines, $\frac{1}{8}" \times \frac{1}{4}" \times 26"$
2. One flat spar, $\frac{1}{8}" \times \frac{1}{4}" \times 22"$
3. Two flat vent sticks: $\frac{3}{16}" \times \frac{1}{4}" \times 6"$
   $\frac{3}{16}" \times \frac{1}{4}" \times 8"$
4. Cover sheet, $26" \times 30"$
5. String and working equipment

FRAME

1. As usual, start by slitting and half-binding all stick ends.
2. Form the spines into an X, shaping the X so that the inter section is $9\frac{1}{2}"$ down from stick ends a and f. Next, adjust stick ends a and f until there is a distance of 8" between their outside edges.
3. Now place the spar horizontally across the spines at the in tersection of the X. Be sure to center the mid-point of the spar on the intersection. Lash the three sticks together and coat the lash ing.
4. Without a doubt both the horizontal line of the spar and the 8" measurement between ends a and f were disturbed during lashing. You'll now need to adjust the sticks accordingly.

TIP: Don't be concerned if the 8" measurement narrows

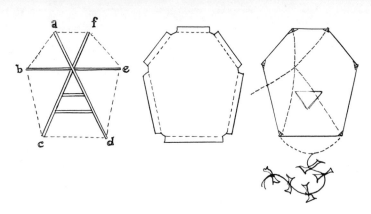

Three-stick Kite

considerably during lashing. You won't bother the lashing when you spread the sticks again. In fact, the spreading will tighten the lashing and make it all the more secure.

5. Frame the entire kite. Once the framing is completed, again check the spar line and the 8″ measurement and carefully make whatever final adjustments are needed. The frame will be complete when you have finished off and coated the bindings at all stick ends.

Tip: If you run into difficulty handling the sticks or keeping them in proper alignment as you work, you can help yourself in two ways:

First, when fashioning the spines into the X, work with the top of the kite toward you and place the tips of the spines flush with the edge of your worktable. This will not only position the upper tips correctly, but will automatically align those at the base of the kite as well. You can then position the spar by checking to see that it is running parallel with the edge of the table.

Second, you can set a book on the sticks or tape them to the table to hold them down during framing. If you use tape, be sure to follow the advice given for the arch-top. Keep the tape well away from the stick ends so that they remain flexible and in no danger of snapping off.

COVER

1. Outline the kite on the cover sheet, using the frame as a guide. Cut out the cover along the overlap, and trim at the stick ends.

2. Before attaching the cover permanently, be sure that the frame is positioned with the spar underneath the spines so that in flight it will be in front of them and thus give the kite maximum strength. Cement the overlap over the framing strings.

3. If you wish, you may vent the kite to give it an extra degree of stability. Prior to attaching the cover, you will need to install a brace for the vent by lashing the vent sticks to the spines as shown in the illustration. Then, once the cover is in place, cut a triangular piece out of it between the vent sticks and reinforce its edges with transparent tape.

BRIDLE AND TAIL

1. The three-sticker needs a four-leg bridle. Stretch the legs from spine ends a, c, d, and f. They should be joined at a point just above the spar-spine intersection and about 10″ out from the face of the kite.

2. To attach the tail, first extend a string in a gentle arc between stick ends c and d. From its mid-point, hang about seven feet worth of line, with bows appropriately spaced. The kite, incidentally, may be flown with two tails, one hanging from each stick at the base of the spine. With the single tail, however, it is a more stable flier.

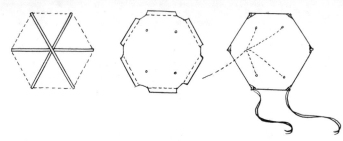

Three-stick Kite with sticks of equal length

A Variation: *The True Hexagon*

As you did with the diamond kite, you can alter the appearance of the three-sticker by using a spar the same length as the spines. Simply lash them together at their mid-points and then spread their tips until the distance between them all is equal. Attach a four-leg bridle at the points shown in the illustration. Why don't you try sticks anywhere from 24″ to 36″ long?

The Star Kite—Five Points

Although the basic three-sticker forms a hexagon, a simple rearrangement of the spines and spar gives a completely different shape—the five-point star. And, as you will see a little later in the chapter, the spar stick can then be bowed to give the kite yet another look—that of a bird. But let's not get ahead of ourselves. For now, let's build the five-point star.

MATERIALS

    1. Two flat spine sticks, ⅛″×¼″×26″
    2. One flat spar stick, ⅛″×¼″×26″
    3. Cover sheet, 30″×30″
    4. String and working equipment

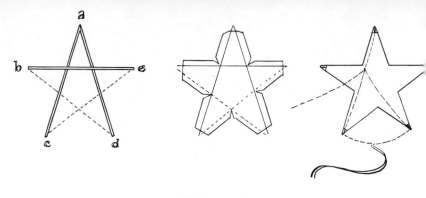

Five-point Star

FRAME

1. Slit and half-bind stick ends b, c, d, and e.

2. Joining the spine sticks at point a, shape them into an up side-down V by spreading them until the distance between the tips at the base of the frame is 15½". The sticks may now be joined at point a in either of two ways:

If you use the method shown on the left in the diagram carve the inner edge of each stick end into a "one-sided" poin about ½" long. Join the spine ends so that they make a singl spear point, glue them together, and then lash securely. A re minder from Chapter 3: shallow notches on the outside edge o each stick will help hold the lashing in place.

Should you decide on the method shown at the right, cut slit about ¾" deep in each stick end. Then cut or saw the woo away on one side of each slit, creating an indentation. Cross th spines in the indentations, then glue and lash them together.

3. Now tie the spar horizontally across the spine sticks 10" down from the top of the frame.

4. When you frame the kite, work with the spar uppermost Run a string between slits b and d, and another between c and e in both cases passing the string *under* the spines. Your kite will be somewhat misshapen if one string passes above and the othe below the spine legs. Finish off your work by tying the framing strings to the spine legs, completing the bindings at the slits, and of course, coating the bindings.

Spine join at point a

COVER

1. Outline the kite, as usual, using the frame as a guide and leaving an overlap of ¾" to 1". When cutting out the cover, trim the overlap at its points and at all stick and string junctions as shown in the illustration.

2. Cement the overlap over the sticks and string. For best results, work from the top of the kite to the bottom.

BRIDLE AND TAIL

1. The five-point star flies well with a three-leg bridle. Extend the legs from stick ends a, c, and d, joining them at a point just above the spar and about 10" out in front of the kite. If by any chance the kite proves unsteady, try bringing additional legs in from b and e. You'll then have a bridle that we haven't seen thus far: the five-legger.

2. As you did with the three-sticker, attach the tail line to the mid-point of a string arcing between c and d. The star, however, does not offer a particularly broad surface and so will need a longer-than-usual tail. For a start, experiment with between fifteen and eighteen feet of line. Because the five-pointer has the look of an oriental kite (especially when imaginatively decorated), you may want to substitute a crepe-paper streamer 1½" wide for the tail line.

SOME VARIATIONS

The star frame of three sticks opens the way to several kites of unusual shape, all of them a challenge to build and a pleasure

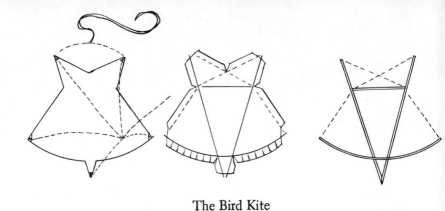

The Bird Kite

to watch in flight. One simple rearrangement of the sticks will give you a six-pointed star. Two other rearrangements will produce models bearing so little resemblance to the star that only you, as the builder, will know that they are based on its frame. For instance, a modification of one stick in the five-pointer will give you:

The Bird Kite

To construct the bird kite, you'll need two flat spines ($\frac{1}{8}'' \times \frac{1}{4}'' \times 26''$), a flexible dowel spar ($\frac{3}{16}'' \times 40''$), and a flat crosspiece ($\frac{1}{8}'' \times \frac{1}{4}'' \times 10''$).

To begin, shape the spines into an upside-down V that leaves a space of 14″ between their base tips. Next, brace the spines with the crosspiece 9″ up from the base tips and lash the spar into place so that its mid-point is 5″ from the top of the kite. To bow the spar, first circle both ends with grooves and then tie a string in each groove. Now draw the strings until each measures 15″ and lash them down, one to each end of the crosspiece. Finally, as shown in the illustration, brace the base tips with additional string.

Fly the kite with a five-leg bridle and a twenty-foot crepe-paper streamer. Try letting the bridle strings meet from 12″ to 15″ out from the kite face, and exactly midway between the spar ends.

The Chinese Hawk

The Chinese Hawk

This kite is particularly interesting to build because, though similar to the bird, it is constructed in two separate pieces. You'll need two flat spines ($\frac{1}{8}'' \times \frac{1}{4}'' \times 24''$), a flexible dowel spar ($\frac{3}{16}'' \times 36''$), and a flat crosspiece ($\frac{1}{8}'' \times \frac{1}{4}'' \times 10''$).

Again, begin by fashioning the spines into a narrow upside-down V, this time leaving a space of 11½" between their base tips. Brace them with the crosspiece as shown in the illustration and then run a framing string between their base tips. Next, shape the dowel into a bowed wing 31" along its base by drawing a string between its two ends. Cover the wing and the V separately and then lash them together so that the mid-point of the wing is down 6" from the top of the kite. You'll need to punch holes in the covers for the lashings; be sure to strengthen each hole with a reinforcing ring.

Fasten a two-leg bridle as shown in the illustration, joining the flying line to it just below the mid-point of the wing and from 12" to 15" out from the face. Finish off by suspending a twenty-foot paper streamer from each spine leg. If the kite proves a little unsteady in the air, switch to a three-leg bridle.

The Six-point Star

You can easily fashion the six-point star with one flat spine (⅛"×¼"×26") and two flat spars (⅛"×¼"×22½").

Simply lash the spars into place 11½" from either end of the spine. Then, following the illustration, frame and cover. At-

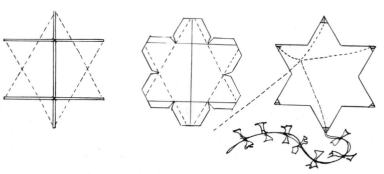

The Six-point Star

:ach a four-leg bridle and a twenty-foot tail line or crepe streamer.
The bridle strings should join from 12″ to 15″ out from the kite
:ace.

The Star—Eight Points

Now, for the last kite in this chapter, let's add a fourth stick.
The result will be the eight-point star, one of the most handsome
of kites.

MATERIALS

1. Four flat sticks, $\frac{1}{8}″ \times \frac{1}{4}″ \times 26″$
2. Cover sheet, 30″×30″
3. String and working equipment

FRAME

1. Slit and half-bind all stick ends.
2. As shown in the illustration, lash all the sticks together at
their mid-points, spreading them until there is an equal distance
between all their tips.
3. The kite must be framed in two steps. First, run a framing
string from a to c-e-g and back to a again. Then, starting at b carry
a second string to d-f-h, returning finally to b. Make certain that
each string passes beneath the intervening sticks. Tie the strings at
the points where they cross the sticks and complete the frame by
finishing off all the slit binds.

COVER

1. Draw an outline of the kite, with the frame serving as a
guide. As usual, draw the outline ¾″ to 1″ oversize.

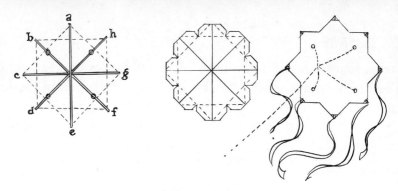

The Eight-point Star

2. As is shown in the illustration, shape the oversize into tabs at the stick ends and the string junctions when cutting out the cover.

3. Cement the cover into place.

BRIDLE AND TAIL

1. You'll need a four-leg bridle. Run the legs from the holes marked on sticks a, d, f, and h, and have them meet at about the center of the face and roughly 10″ out from it.

2. The eight-pointer flies best with five tails. Try about fifteen feet of crepe streamer from stick end e, with shorter tails from d and f, and still shorter ones from c and g. You'll have to experiment a bit before finding just the right lengths for each set.

All right. With the flat kite in its various shapes, you've had a good chance to develop your kite-making skills. The flat kite may please you so much that you'll want to stay with it for the rest of your flying days. But if you want to move on to more complex kites, now is the moment to do so. Next, we begin building the bow kite.

5
THE BOW KITE

As you already know, the bow kite flies more stably and with less drag than its flat-faced brother. It does so because of the aerodynamic shape called dihedral. Dihedral, which is found in the bird wing and in many an aircraft wing, is defined as the "angle formed at the meeting of two supporting planes." In the bow kite, that angle is formed by arching the spar back into a shallow V from its join with the spine.

Dihedral reduces drag by "streamlining" the kite face; it simply pulls the face back on either side of the spine and cuts down the amount of wind resistance exerted by the cover material. At the same time, it creates stabilizing "pockets" in the face. These pockets, which can be described as "caved-in" cheeks, are areas of slack cover material to either side of the spine. They catch the air in such a way as to hold the kite headed into the wind and safe from a sideways slip, a trick that the flat kite likes to try all too often. Here's how they work:

Imagine that you're looking straight down on the kite as it is facing into the wind. Now suppose a sudden gust strikes the left side, pushing it back and driving the right side forward. The flat kite would likely slip completely sideways and dip out of control, but here, as the right side rides forward, it catches the air particles in its pocket and slows their movement. There is an immediate in-

Dihedral

crease in their pressure. They ease the right side back into place, stabilizing the kite and facing it into the wind again.

It is this stabilizing action that, as was said in Chapter 2, makes a tail line unnecessary for most bow kites. In fact, there are only two reasons for attaching a tail to certain bows, chief among them the excellent Eddy kite. You have not constructed the kite so that it is in perfect balance. Or you want the tail line for decoration.

Drawing the Bowstring

In the basic two-sticker, the bow is made by drawing a string between the tips of the spar; in kites of an unusual design, such as the hexagon, additional bowstrings will be needed, sometimes one for each of the sticks. The string is to be drawn until the bow reaches the desired *depth*—the distance between the string itself and the mid-point of the stick. The distance will vary according to kite size and day-to-day flying conditions, but it should never be particularly deep; a too-deep bow turns all the rules of dihedral around and reduces lift.

Kites about three feet long do well with bows three or four inches deep, while six-footers usually require a depth of no more than six inches. You'll need to experiment a bit to find the right

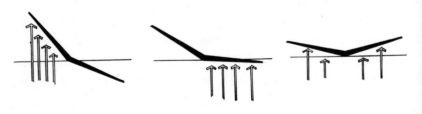

Dihedral at work

depth for a given kite and a given wind. One point will help: Slightly deeper bows are needed for heavier winds.

The bow should always be made so that its arch is facing forward into the wind. Choose a flexible, well-balanced stick for the job and, of course, slit it at either end. You can make the stick more "bendable" if you soak it in water for a few moments beforehand. Then tie the bowstring to one slit and draw the string across to the opposite slit, shaping the arch as you go. Take care to see that the rising curves on either side of the spine are identical. Tie the string off when the bow is of the desired depth.

Knotting the Bowstring

It's a good idea to prepare the bowstring with knotted loops at either end before getting down to work. In this way, you won't need to do your knotting while handling the stick. Simply cut a piece of string to the appropriate length, shape each end with a loop, insert one loop into one slit, and gently arch the stick until the other loop can be slipped into place.

What of the string length that needs to be cut? Exactly how long should it be in relation to stick length? Much depends on the depth of bow wanted, but for the conventional-sized kite, try a string about six inches longer than the stick and then shape the knots so that their loops are three inches long. Small kites usually require a string proportionally longer, while the lengths for large kites are proportionally shorter—sometimes the same length as the stick. As usual, a little experimentation will show you what is needed.

Rather than inserting the looped ends directly into the slits, some kite makers prefer to use the "S" hook arrangement shown here. One leg of the hook is bound in the slit, and the other accepts the bowstring. The hooks can be made of strong wire.

Bowstring hooks

Your First Bow Kites

In common with the flat kite, the bow can be fashioned in a variety of shapes. In fact, if you wish, you may construct your first bows simply by modifying several of the kites in Chapter 4.

For a start, try converting the flat two-sticker into a bow. Just draw a string between the spar tips. Best here is a bow depth of three or four inches. A two-leg bridle will do nicely. Test the kite to see if it will get by without a tail line.

The hexagon that was made of sticks all of the same length can be converted by arching each stick to a depth of three or four inches and tying all the bowstrings together at the point where they intersect. As a bow, the hexagon becomes the interestingly shaped "umbrella" kite. It takes the same bridle as the flat version and should, if all sticks are identically bowed, fly without a tail. You'll probably want to attach a short tail line when the wind is

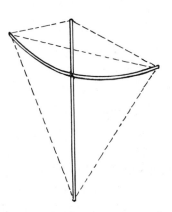

Two-stick Bow Kite

strong, for then the "umbrella" likes to bounce about like a cork in rough water.

The frame used for the six-point star can, with a slight change in stick lengths, become your first "airplane kite."

For the airplane, use two flat sticks ⅛"×¼"×22" for the spine and upper spar; a third flat stick (⅛"×¼") between 10" and 12" long will do fine for the lower spar. Lash the sticks together, as shown in the illustration, and then frame them, letting the framing string cross the spine just above the lower spar. Both the upper and lower spar should be bowed to a depth of 2½".

The kite is to be covered in two steps—first the large diamond formed by the spine and upper spar, and then the small diamond below. The outline of an airplane on the cover gives the kite its final look. The "plane" should soar along nicely with a two-leg bridle and without a tail line. You might want to try a plastic streamer to give a contrail effect.

With yet another change in stick dimensions, the six-point frame will give you a conventional-sized version of the kite that Baden-Powell constructed to carry a man aloft. It is known variously as the double-bow kite or the Baden-Powell levitor.

Three dowels or flat sticks, each 36" long, will be needed. If you choose dowels, their diameters should be ¼" or ³⁄₁₆"; flat sticks should be at least ⅛"×⅜". Lash the spars to the spine at their mid-points, 6¼" from the top and bottom of the kite. Frame, attach the cover, and bow each spar to a 3" or 4" depth. Either a two- or three-leg bridle will serve well. The two-legger is best tied to the top of the spine and the mid-point of the lower spar. The three-legger is attached as shown in the illustration; the upper legs should come from points 10" to either side of the spine. For a start, have the bridle legs meet 15" out from the face and just below the upper spar.

The levitor, incidentally, may also be constructed as a flat kite. Bowed, it usually needs no tail. Flat, it will probably want a tail line around 9' long.

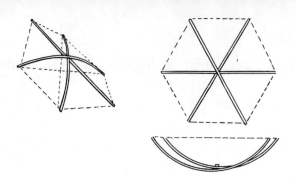

Hexagon Bow Kite (Umbrella Kite)

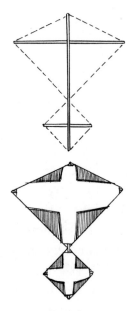

Airplane Kite

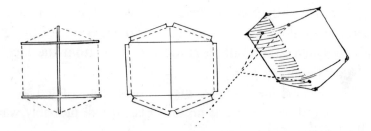

Double Bow Kite (Baden-Powell Levitor)

The basic three-sticker can also be converted into a bow—one of the most interesting bows that you'll probably ever see. But the job is a shade on the complicated side, and so we'll save it for a few moments. In the meantime, let's look at what many builders and fliers think to be the finest of all bows—the Eddy kite. It is so stable that, unless poorly constructed and balanced, it is guaranteed to fly without a tail.

The Eddy Kite

The kite is named for its nineteenth-century inventor, William A. Eddy, a New Jersey journalist and kite maker. In the early 1890s, tired of having the various tail lines in his kite trains tangle in the flying lines, he set about developing a highly stable tailless kite. Several years went into the project, and his final design did not take shape until he happened to see a number of Malayan tailless kites on display at Chicago's Columbian Exposition. Today, his kite, which he patented in 1897, is said to be the most popular bow in America.

The Eddy kite is built with two sticks of equal length. It adapts itself easily to a variety of sizes. Though usually seen in three- or four-foot lengths, it can be scaled up to a giant with a spine of eight feet or more. Let's try our hand with an Eddy of conventional size.

MATERIALS

1. One flat spine, $\frac{1}{8}'' \times \frac{3}{8}'' \times 36''$
2. One flat spar, $\frac{1}{8}'' \times \frac{3}{8}'' \times 36''$
3. One flat spar support, $\frac{1}{8}'' \times \frac{3}{8}'' \times 12''$
4. Cover material, $40'' \times 40''$
5. String and working equipment

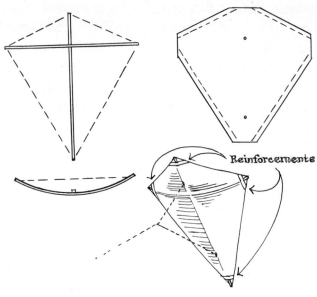

Reinforcements

The Eddy Kite

FRAME

1. As usual, slit and half-bind all spine and spar tips.

2. The spar takes a great deal of strain and so should be reinforced by gluing and lashing it to the support stick. Make certain that the mid-point of the support stick is placed directly atop the mid-point of the spar; otherwise, the kite will be out of balance. The support stick here is 12″ long, or one-third the length of the spar. When building a larger Eddy, you'll need to increase the support stick length; always cut it one-third as long as the spar.

3. Lash the spine and spar at right angles 8½″ down from the top of the kite. This distance will increase proportionately when larger versions are built. In the six-footer, for instance, the intersection will be set 15″ from the kite top.

4. Frame the kite with string and complete the binds at the stick ends.

COVER

1. Draw an outline of the cover, making it the usual oversize. When you have cut out the cover and cemented it into place, you may wish to reinforce its edges at all stick ends. Reinforcements here will help protect the edges from tearing when the pockets are pushed in by the wind. The reinforcements, which are shown in the illustration, may be made of thin cloth or transparent-tape strips.

2. Bow the spar to a 3" depth.

BRIDLE AND TAIL

1. The Eddy kite is ordinarily flown with a two-leg bridle. The bridle may be attached in either of two ways. You may extend the legs from holes 5" from the top and 8" from the bottom of the kite (as shown in the illustration), or from the spine-spar join and the point 8" from the bottom. In either case, join the legs about 13" out from the face and then, if necessary, make adjustments during your test flights.

2. The Eddy, of course, is designed to fly without a tail—and will do so if built in proper balance. For decorative purposes, however, you may hang a crepe streamer from its spine, adding shorter lengths to its spar ends if you wish. Some fliers like to festoon the top of the spine with a small pennant or flag.

VARIATIONS

An Eddy with a somewhat "different" look can be had with the addition of a third stick. The kite may then be given a converging spine, as seen on the left of the illustration, or a parallel spine.

As with the basic Eddy, each variation requires that all sticks

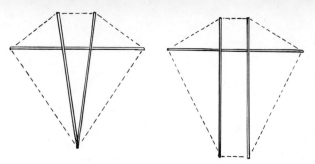

Converging- and parallel-spine Eddy Kites

be of equal length. With 36″ sticks, the converging spines should
be built in a narrow V that leaves a gap of 9″ at the top; the spines
should run side-by-side and 9″ apart in the parallel version.

The converging-spine Eddy is flown from a three-leg bridle,
with the legs attached to the points formed by the ends of the V.
You'll need a four-leg bridle for the parallel spine. The legs come
in to meet from the top and bottom of each spine.

The Flat-nose Kite

Now, as promised, it's time to convert the basic three-sticker
into a bow. And, as promised, the kite will be one of the most unusual bows you'll ever build. It is known as the flat-nose kite or the
flat-nose three-sticker.

Up to this point, we've been making kites that are back-
bowed, meaning, of course, that the spar is fastened to the spine
and then arched back. With the three-sticker, we turn to the forward bow. The spar is still bowed with its tips to the rear, but it is
no longer tied to the spine; rather, it rides free and to the front of
the spine, in this way giving the kite its "flat-nosed" look. As for
the spine itself, it is tied to the bowstring. In general, as seen from
the top, the whole arrangement looks like the illustration below.

Got it? Good. Now let's build the three-sticker.

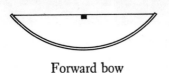

Forward bow

MATERIALS

1. Two flat spines, ⅛″×⅜″×36″
2. One flat spar, ⅛″×⅜″×36″
3. Cover material, 32″×40″
4. String and working equipment

FRAME

1. Slit and half-bind all stick ends.

2. As you did with the basic three-sticker, cross and lash the spines together in a narrow X, intersecting them at a point 10½″ down from their tops and positioning them so that their base tips are 19″ apart.

3. Next, bow the spar until the bowstring is 26″ long. Now tie the mid-point of the bowstring to the spinal intersection. For the moment, just let the arched spar hang in front of the spines.

4. To frame the kite, place the skeleton on your worktable, with the spar beneath the spine. Make certain that the bowstring is running out straight to either side of the intersection and then circle the kite with framing string, inserting it in each slit as you go. Finish off by completing the binds at the stick ends.

COVER

1. Because of the strain that the bowed spar will soon put on it, the cover material really should be a lightweight cloth and should be attached according to the instructions at the end of this chapter. If paper is your choice, make your selection carefully, cut it with the usual overlap, trim at the stick ends, and cement into place.

2. Once the cover is attached, gently—very gently—push the

spar forward into the face until the mid-point of the arch is thrusting out directly ahead of the spinal intersection. In all, it's now an odd-looking kite, but you'll find that it flies nicely, especially in a light breeze.

BRIDLE AND TAIL

1. The flat nose is customarily flown with a variation of the three-leg bridle. The variation, which is shown in the illustration, consists of two legs rising from the base tips of the spines, with the third leg coming down in a Y from the top of the kite. The legs should meet about a quarter of the way down—and 12" out— from the face.

2. Ordinarily, a tail line is not needed. Decorative streamers from the base of each spine are quite attractive, though.

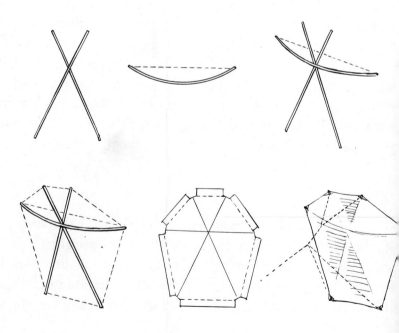

The Flat-nose Kite

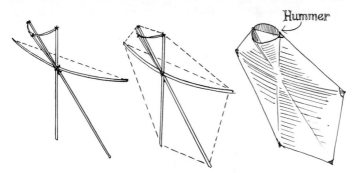

Hummer

Flat-nose Head-stick Kite

A VARIATION

The flat nose can be converted into an even more unusual kite—and a pleasantly noisy one—by adding a short stick (called a head stick) and a thin bamboo strip. They turn it into the flat-nose head-stick kite.

Choose a head stick of the same width and thickness as the spar and spines, but one just long enough to extend straight up from the intersection to a point level with the upper spine tips. Lash it to the intersection and then bow a bamboo strip between the upper spine tips. The bamboo should be bowed about 3″ deep toward the front of the kite, with the head stick then to be inclined forward and lashed to the strip.

What about noise? As shown in the illustration, fold a curved paper flap over the framing string at the top of the kite and cement it into place. The wind will catch the flap, causing it to hum. Flaps such as this—or short lengths of paper—can be attached to many kites. They're all known as "hummers" or "buzzers."

The kite is best flown with a six-leg bridle. The legs, coming from all the spar and spine ends, should meet about 6″ in front of the intersection.

The three-sticker is not the only kite able to accept a forward bow. You might one day want to try a forward bow in your two-stick trapezoid or your Baden-Powell levitor. If so, just follow the following diagrams.

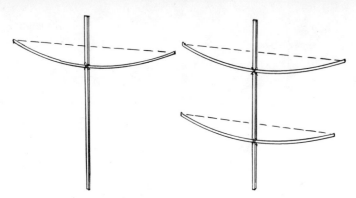

Forward-bowed, Two-stick, and Levitor Kites

The Rectangular Kite

Thus far, we've worked with four sticks at the most. Now we're going to make a sudden jump to ten. With them, we'll build the rectangular kite.

It is a kite that, on three counts, appeals to many builders. First, if properly made, it flies stably. Second, it offers a broad face that invites imaginative decoration. The cover can be entirely filled with an animal or human face if you wish. Or you might try a human figure, such as a knight of old or an oriental warrior. Or you can choose an abstract design. The rectangular kite is one of the standard models flown in Japan, and so you'll often see it painted with an oriental motif.

Finally, the kite promises an interesting "change of pace" for the builder. The skeleton goes together in its own way. The framing string is easily installed, but in a manner distinct from that used for most other kites. And the cover requires a special method of attachment. In all, the rectangle offers a great challenge—but a highly enjoyable one.

MATERIALS

1. Three vertical flat ribs, ⅛"×⅜"×28"
2. Two horizontal flat ribs, ⅛"×⅜"×24"

3. Three horizontal flat ribs, ⅛"×⅜"×22"
4. Two flat diagonal ribs, ⅛"×⅜"×38"
5. Cover sheet, 28"×32"
6. String and working equipment

FRAME

1. For the rectangular kite, you need not cut slits into any of the stick ends. Rather, your first job is to arrange the ribs into the latticelike skeleton shown in the illustration. Each stick should be carefully set in place so that the "panes" all equal each other in size. Each pane (a) should be slightly longer than it is wide.

2. Once you have the ribs properly arranged, glue and tie all the sticks together. So that the skeleton won't be disturbed as you work, it's a good idea to anchor all intersecting points with strips of tape (b) before starting. The strips are then removed, one at a time, and replaced with a glue-and-string lashing.

3. You may find the join at the center of the kite—four sticks deep—a little too thick and unwieldy for comfortable handling. If so, groove the crosspoints just slightly with sandpaper or a file. They'll then lock together more securely. But put the accent on *slightly*. Don't make the grooves too deep—and don't crosscut the sticks. The center join carries much strain and must not be unduly weakened.

4. Check to see how far the diagonal ribs jut out from the corners of the kite. To avoid the possibility of error, the length specified for the diagonals (38") was put on the generous side. If the tips extend too far out from the corners, trim them back until they match with the tips in the illustration.

5. You'll need to frame the kite in two steps. Tie a framing string to one top corner, carry it down to a point about 1" inside the end of the first short horizontal rib, loop it around the rib (c),

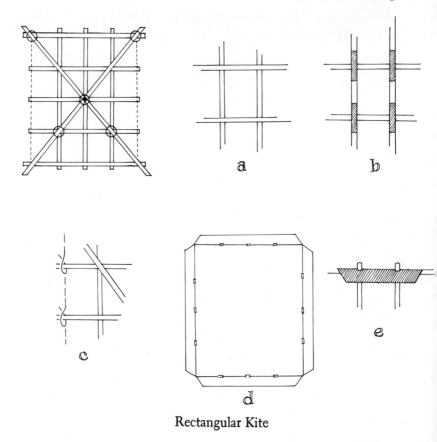

Rectangular Kite

and continue on your way, looping it around each successive rib as you go until you can tie off at the bottom corner. Repeat the process on the opposite side of the skeleton.

COVER

1. The cover (d) must be made so that its oversize folds over the framing strings and the top and bottom ribs; all rib endings must protrude through the paper. Using the frame as a guide, you can insure a proper fit by drawing two outlines on the cover. The

first should follow the outside edges of the framing strings and the top and bottom ribs. The second, which will give you the necessary oversize, can be run along a line even with the ends of the longest sticks.

2. Cut out the cover along the larger outline and divide the oversize into flaps by notching V's at all corners; have the points of the V's touch the corners of the smaller outline. Now fold the flaps over along the smaller outline and, again using the frame as a guide, mark and cut slits in the cover at all points corresponding with the stick ends.

3. When attaching the cover, work from the top of the kite and with the frame so placed that the diagonal ribs are against the paper. Slip the protruding rib ends through the slits (e) and cement the flap to the horizontal rib. Now cover the framing string at your right, then at your left, and finish off with the bottom rib. Throughout, work carefully, always easing the rib ends through the slits. Haste is sure to rip the paper.

4. Bow the top and bottom horizontal ribs to a slight depth, making certain that you do not put too much strain on the sticks. Final bowing will depend a great deal on wind conditions.

BRIDLE AND TAIL

1. A five-leg bridle should be attached at the circled points shown in the illustration. Have the legs meet level with the midpoint of the first horizontal rib down from the top. You'll find yourself cutting long legs, for they should join in front of the kite at a distance at least the length of the frame.

2. The kite is able to fly without a tail, but sometimes does best with lines from either side of its base. Why don't you try 1½"- or ·2"-wide crepe streamers? Let each be two or three times as long as the kite is diagonal.

Attaching a Cloth Cover

As said earlier, a durable and "stretchable" paper (crepe paper is a good choice) can be safely used as a cover for most bow kites of a conventional size. But, because the face must have a fair degree of "give" in the pocket areas so that they can handle the wind without ripping, the bow really is best covered with plastic or a lightweight cloth.

Should you go to cloth, don't forget that your method of covering will be quite different than that used with paper. Let's talk about it now.

When you use cloth, you do not frame the sticks prior to covering. Rather, you frame the *cover* and then attach it and framing string to the sticks in a single operation. To begin, cut the cloth in an outline of the kite, adding the usual ¾" to 1" oversize. Next, fold the oversize back to bring the cover to its actual size. It's a good idea to pin the folded oversize into place, for your next step is to set the cover on the sticks and trim away all corners so that the cloth is about ½" from the stick ends. This will keep the cloth from overlapping the stick ends when the cover is finally attached.

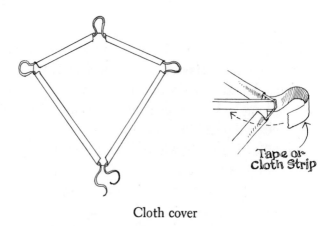

Cloth cover

Now hem the cloth all along its edges. Make sure that none of the hems are sewn closed at their ends, for you next must use them as "tunnels," threading the framing string through them. Start and end the threading at the bottom of the cover and leave the string looped at all corners.

The job's almost done. Once the cover is framed, place it on the sticks and draw the string ends at the bottom until the loops disappear and the strings at the corners settle into the stick-end slits. Tie off the string ends and bind all the slits. And that's it.

One additional point: Prior to attachment, strips of cloth tape should be sewn to all corners. You must then tape or lash them to the stick ends when the cover is in place. The wind will always want to pull the cover edges along the framing string and away from the corners. The strips will anchor the cloth to the corners.

You've met many a challenge in this and the previous chapter, and your collection of kites should be fast becoming the envy of the neighborhood. And your kite-making skills should be growing and sharpening daily. Ready now to add further to your collection and your skills? Ready to try your hand at the box kite?

If so, the next chapter is for you.

6

THE BOX KITE

Thanks to its stability and its talent for carrying heavy loads, the box kite was long ago named the "workhorse of kiting." Through the years since its invention in 1893, kite men have found numerous "donkey" jobs for it. Meteorologists have sent it aloft with recording equipment to check the atmosphere. Photographers have tied cameras to it. Politicians have flown campaign banners from it, and Fourth-of-July celebrants have launched it as a "space platform" for aerial fireworks. Early in this century, one young man suspended a lantern from his newly made box kite and unwittingly frightened the people of a small California farm town. They were certain they were seeing a heavenly visitor in the night sky—their first UFO.

Though a workhorse, the box kite is anything but a dullard. As a flier, you'll find that it likes to fly in trains or in tandem. You'll learn that, in certain winds, it is quite likely to abandon its stable ways and become as skitterish as a kitten, demanding that you put all your flying skills to work. And you'll discover that it flies well at any reasonable size. Just one word of caution, however: If yours is a giant version, be sure to take a friend along on your flying sessions. When six feet or longer, the box becomes a two-man kite.

As a builder, you'll be able to construct the box in three basic shapes and then modify them into even more interesting-looking kites. Each box may be built with flat sticks, dowels, or bamboo strips; flat sticks and bamboo sticks should all be as straight and as well-balanced as possible. Each box may be covered with paper, cloth, or plastic, with cloth and plastic being your best bets for models of larger-than-average size. Most boxes may be made with either a rigid frame (all members permanently locked in place) or a collapsible one for easy storage and transport.

The basic shapes for the box kite are the square-cell, the oblong, and the triangle. We'll build them all first and then look at the modifications that can be made for greater interest. All our directions will be for kites of a rigid frame. Late in the chapter we'll talk about how collapsible frames are made.

Ready? Here we go.

The Square-celled Box Kite

This is the most basic of the box kites. It consists of a papered section (cell) at each end, with a stretch of exposed spine sticks in between. Though forming a rectangle when looked at from the side, it is called the "square-celled" box kite because, with its spines all equidistant, it divides itself into three squares when papered—two covered cells and one open one.

MATERIALS

1. Four flat spines, ¼"×⅜"×36"
2. Eight flat crosspieces, ¼"×⅜"×12½"
3. Four flat bracing sticks, ¼"×⅜"×19"
4. Two cover sheets, each 15"×52"
5. String and working equipment

FRAME

1. Your first job is to make the crosspieces into two "panes," each 12" square (a). The members in each pane will eventually

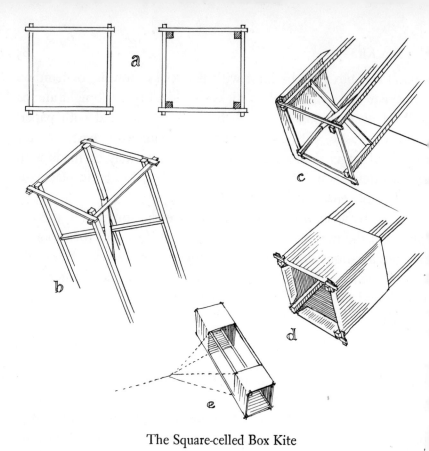

The Square-celled Box Kite

need to be lashed together, but for the moment simply glue them into place as shown in the illustration.

2. Once the glue has dried, assemble the box frame by extending the spines from one pane to the other (b). Glue each spine to its appropriate corner in each pane. Finish off your work by lashing each spine to its crosspieces.

3. Now the kite must be braced to firm the skeleton. Two braces (b) are needed. Each is made by lashing two sticks together in an X and notching their ends so that they correspond with the edges of the spines. As usual, to avoid the possibility of error, the measurements given for the braces were set on the generous side, and so each stick will first need to be trimmed somewhat;

String brace

a length of about 17″ should give you a snug fit. Install the braces about 6″ from either end of the kite. At those points, they will be hidden by the cover panels. The braces should be glued and lashed in place.

Tip: The box kite is said to perform at its best when there is as much open space as possible within its skeleton. Consequently, many kite makers frown on the stick brace, thinking that even the narrow widths of the wood interfere with the air flow. They advise that a string brace be used instead. It is fashioned by drawing a string between three of the spines as shown. The string should be wrapped two or three times around each spine and then secured with glue.

4. Now, at points 12″ along the spine from the top and bottom of the kite carry framing strings all around the skeleton (b), looping them around each stick as you go. These strings will serve, along with the crosspieces, as anchor lines for the covers.

COVER

1. As is shown in the illustration (c), establish each cell by stretching the paper around the spines and cementing it into place when it returns to its starting point. It's a good idea to cement the paper to each stick as you come to it. Be careful to keep the paper running in a straight line as you circle the kite. And pull it as taut as possible. For best flying, the covers need to be very tight.

2. When the paper is finally in place, trim it into V's at each

corner of the cells. Then fold it back over the crosspieces and the framing strings, cementing it down (d). One cell should be completely finished off before the other is started. Cement the paper to the crosspieces first, and then to the framing strings.

TIP: If you are using a cloth cover, do not attach the framing strings to the kite beforehand. Rather, hem each panel along one of its edges and then thread the string through the hem, after which the panel can be attached. The "unhemmed" edge of the cloth will then have to be folded over the crosspieces and stitched into place.

BRIDLE

1. The square-celled kite may be flown from a two- or four-leg bridle (e). No matter which you choose, extend the legs from a point 4" from the top of one cell and from the edge of the other. They should join just below the paper edge of the upper cell. You'll need to experiment a bit to find the best distance out from the kite face for the bridle join. For a start, try upper and lower bridle legs that together measure from 28" to 30".

2. The kite may also be flown from a one-leg bridle. Just attach the flying line to one of the spines at the bottom edge of the upper cover.

When rigged with a one- or two-leg bridle, the kite will fly with one spine angled into the wind. With a four-legger, it will lie somewhat flat to the horizon, with one side facing earthward. Angled, the kite has greater stability. Flat, it produces greater lift.

The Oblong Box Kite

The oblong kite differs from its square-celled brother in two respects. First, when seen from the end, it does not form a square.

Second, when seen from the side, it presents cover panels of two different sizes, one at least twice as wide as the other.

MATERIALS

1. Four flat spines, ¼"×⅜"×36"
2. Four flat crosspieces, ¼"×⅜"×24"
3. Four flat crosspieces, ¼"×⅜"×7½"
4. Two flat bracing sticks, ¼"×⅜"×27"
5. Two cover sheets, 12"×66" and 22"×66"
6. String and working equipment

FRAME

1. Begin just as you did with the square-cell, this time gluing together two panes that are 24" long and 7" wide (a). Let the glue dry before taking your next step.

2. Again, as with the square-cell, assemble the skeleton by connecting the spines to the panes and making the kite into a tall, narrow box (b). The spines should be glued and lashed into place, after which the framing strings can be installed. Run one string around the kite 9" from the top, the other 19" from the bottom. Remember to loop the strings around the spines as you go.

3. As before, lash the bracing sticks (b) together in an X, measure them to fit the skeleton (again, their lengths are on the generous side), and notch them at their ends so that they fit snugly against the spines. The brace should be installed midway down the kite, where it will be hidden by the larger of the cover panels. It should be glued and lashed in place. If you wish, you many use the string brace instead.

COVER

1. As is to be expected, attach the cover just as if you were working with the square-cell, wrapping the paper around the skele-

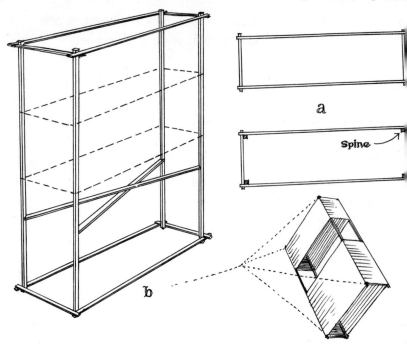

The Oblong Box Kite

ton, trimming it into V's at all corners, and cementing it over the crosspieces and the framing strings. Don't forget to draw the paper as taut as possible.

BRIDLE

1. A four-legger is the only bridle that can be used with the oblong, for if the kite is to rise, it must have one of its broad side facing into the wind. The kite always flies with its narrow pane uppermost, and with the bridle legs coming from the top corner of each cell. The towing point is just beneath the lower edge of the small panel. As for distance out from the kite face: Again, try having each set of bridle legs equal 28″ to 30″ overall. Flight performance will indicate needed adjustments.

The Triangular Box Kite

To some kite men, the triangular box, with its crosspieces angling into one of its spines, is the "flying roof." Because of those angled crosspieces you'll find the triangle a challenge for your model-making skills. Adding further to the challenge is the fact that the triangle is best built with dowels.

MATERIALS

1. Three dowel spines, ¼"×36"
2. Six dowel crosspieces, ¼"×12"
3. Two cover sheets, 14"×40"
4. String and working equipment

FRAME

1. Your first job is to carve the ends of all the crosspieces so that they will hug the spines (a). Don't forget to add the grooves shown in the illustration. Have them circle each dowel end to a depth sufficient to hold three or four turns of string.

2. Now mark each spine 5" in from each end and attach the crosspieces at the marks. This will give you the "peaked roof" skeleton (b). The crosspieces should first be glued to the spines. Once the glue is dry lash all the joins with string or a strong thread.

3. Finally, frame the skeleton with string at four points—at each end and 11" in from each end (c). The strings, of course, will serve as anchor lines for the covers.

COVER

1. Attach the covers (d) just as you did before. Be sure to

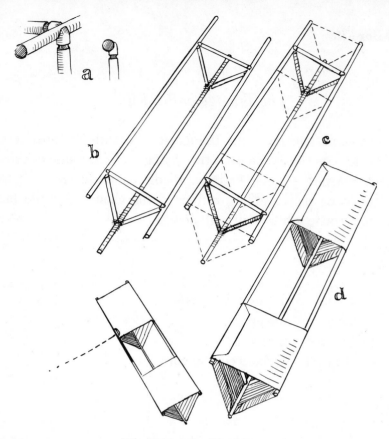

The Triangular Box Kite

draw the paper taut. And be sure to carry it around the kite in a straight line.

BRIDLE

1. You may attach a one- or two-leg bridle. Fasten the one-legger to the spine at the lower edge of the top panel. For the two-legger, bring the cords from the top of the kite and the upper edge of the bottom cell; again, try legs whose overall length is about 30″.

There. Now you have the three basic box kites. In a moment, we'll talk about the variations possible. But first—

COLLAPSIBLE FRAMES

The box kites we've made thus far have rigid frames. All members are glued and lashed permanently into place. Built this way, the kites are exceptionally strong, but they are also something of a headache. They take up much space when stored and prove a clumsy nuisance when being carried out to your favorite flying grounds. As soon as you've built your first rigid frame, you'll know the problem of fitting it into your closet, mounting it on your bike, or easing it into the back seat or trunk of a compact car.

The whole problem can be avoided with a collapsible frame. It is built with braces that can be removed after flying, enabling the kite to fold in on itself along its length. It can then be easily carried by hand or inserted in a mailing tube for safekeeping.

The collapsible frame, however, requires a different building technique. In fact, the entire construction process is reversed. Rather than putting the sticks together and then attaching the covers, you begin with the covers and then cement the sticks to them. Shall we give it a try?

Let's say that you're building the square-celled kite. It's to have two cells, each 12″ square, and so you'll need cover panels 15″ wide and 52″ long. As shown (a), set out each panel, trim it at the ends, and mark fold lines 1½″ in all along either side. Place strings along the lines and then fold and cement the cover edges over them. (Of course, if you are using cloth, stitch rather than cement the folds into place.) The strings should be about 4″ longer than the length of the panel and should dangle free at either end. They'll later be used for tying the panel ends together.

Now, beginning 2″ in from either end, draw a series of five lines (b) across each panel, setting the lines at 12″ intervals. Next, position the spines on the first four lines (c) and cement (sew if using cloth) them to the panels. As shown, let the stick ends protrude about 1″ beyond the outer edge of each panel.

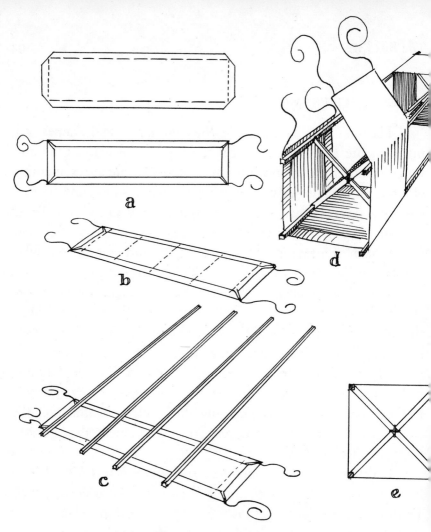

Collapsible frame construction procedure

Finally, shape the spines and panels into a box (d), cement (or sew) the end flaps together, and tie off the strings. To firm the box, use two cross braces (e), positioning them inside the cells. The braces may be lashed together with string or a rubber band. They should be carefully measured so that they fit snugly, and their ends should be notched to hug the spines.

The procedure for building the oblong and the triangular kite is essentially the same. The triangle, however, will need a three-leg brace. It consists of a center piece and three dowels.

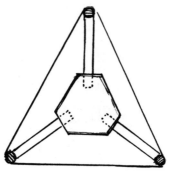

Three-leg brace

The center piece is easily shaped from a bit of wood. Holes are drilled at appropriate points to hold the dowels. It is not necessary to glue the dowels in the holes; tension will hold them in place, and the brace can then be taken apart between flights. The dowel ends should be carved to fit snugly against the spines.

VARIATIONS

Now let's look at the imaginative ways in which builders through the years have varied the design of the box kite. The result has been a series of entertaining and interesting-looking kites. You'll be able to match these variations by adding from one to four sticks to your list of materials. For instance, the addition of two sticks to the square-celled box will give you the unusual:

Hexagon Box Kite

The hexagon is best built with a collapsible frame. It should be braced with sticks running diagonally between the spines. You may fly it with a two- or four-leg bridle.

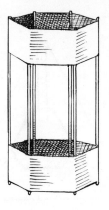

The Hexagon Box Kite

After trying this first variation, you might want to see what can be done with the oblong and the triangle. One kite that blends the features of both is:

The Flying Wedge

To build a flying wedge of conventional size, use sticks 36″ long for the uprights; let the front and back base sticks measure 24″ each, and the side sticks 12″ each. The triangle in the face of the kite may be framed with sticks or a strong lightweight cord. It begins 9″ down from the top.

When the kite is papered, the sides and the facial triangle are left open. To cover, begin at the top of the facial triangle and carry the paper up over the crown, then down the back, and across the bottom. Panels fitting the sides of the facial triangle should then be cut and cemented into place.

The wedge flies with its face into the wind and its narrow edge at the top. It needs a three-leg bridle, with the legs coming from the points of the facial triangle. And, unlike other box kites, it will probably need a tail when flown by itself; try attaching 1½″ to 2″ streamers from its lower front corners. The wedge performs best in tandem with a fellow wedge. More about tandem flying in a later chapter.

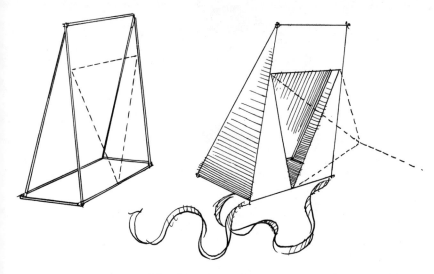

The Flying-wedge Kite

Wings have always been a welcome addition to the box kite —welcome because they increase its lifting power. They can be fitted to both the square-celled and triangular boxes. Simple wing attachments will give you the following kites.

The Winged Square-celled Box Kite

This wing model takes shape when a spar is placed diagonally across the square-celled kite. The spar, which is lashed into place at the base of the upper cell, should ride out 11″ or 12″ from either side of the kite.

Each wing is framed with string that runs from the top of the adjacent spine to the end slit in the spar and on to the base of the spine. The covers are then cemented to the strings and the spines. If you make a collapsible skeleton, do not fully bind the end slits in the spar, but use half-binds instead. You'll then be able to free the spar easily from its framing strings so that it can be removed from the kite; of course, the lashings at the spines will have to be cut and new ones made when next you fly. Once the spar is re-

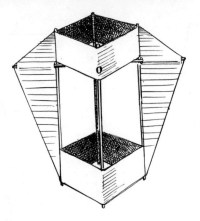

The Winged Square-celled Box Kite

moved, the kite—with the wing coverings still attached—can be rolled up for storage.

The kite is best flown with a one-leg bridle when the wind is light to medium; attach it to a point about two inches up from the base of the top panel. If the wind is high, switch to a two-legger, attaching it to the points suggested for the basic square-celled box. And get ready for some fun—the kite tugs with tremendous force in heavy weather.

The Military Kite

Given its name because several nations once tried to use it for military observation, the kite is made by attaching four spars to your square-celled frame. For a 3′-long frame, the spars should each run 30″ and should be crisscrossed at the top and bottom of the kite. They must not be crossed at their exact mid-points, but must be set so that the wings to the rear will be wider than those up front. Each rear wing should have a span of 9″. Each front wing will then automatically have a 4″ span.

After lashing down the spars at all points where they join with the spines, frame each wing with string all along its outer length, and then cement the covers into place. If the kite frame is

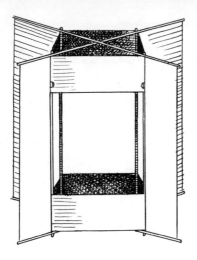

The Military Kite

rigid, cement the covers to the spines, the framing strings, *and* the spars. If the frame is flexible, avoid cementing the covers directly to the spars. Rather, as shown in the illustration, cement the paper into loops within which the spars will fit. The spars can then be withdrawn when the time comes to "break the kite down" for the trip home. As with the winged square-cell, you'll also need to cut the lashings at the spine.

The military kite is flown with a two-leg bridle attached at the points indicated in the illustration. It is a fine flier, one that the Germans built to a giant size during World War I for the purpose of sending observers aloft from submarines. The effort never went beyond the experimental stage, but even then, some men were lifted as high as one hundred feet.

The Conyne Kite

Born in 1902 and named for its Chicago inventor, Silas J. Conyne, this is one of the finest of kites. It is blessed with stability and great lift and is built by adding a spar to the back of the triangular box kite. The spar, which should be the same length as the spines, is lashed across the base of the upper cell.

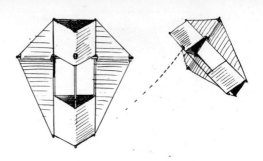

The Conyne Kite

The spar is framed in the same manner as the winged square cell, with the paper then cemented to the framing strings and the adjacent spines. If your skeleton is collapsible, be sure just to half-bind the spar slits so that the spar can be easily removed.

You may also bow the spar to a slight depth is you wish to add to the kite's already-great lifting power. You'll find that the kite behaves well with a one- or two-leg bridle. For a start, if the kite is 3' long, anchor the one-legger to the front spine (the keel) about 7½" down from the top of the upper panel. The two-legger should be attached about 5" from the top and bottom of the keel. Bridle lengths and the best point of attachment with the flying line will be much determined by the wind. You'll need to experiment a bit to find just the right lengths and setting.

Early in this century, the French experimented with the Conyne kite as a "floating platform" for military observation. Their experiments became so identified with the Conyne that it was eventually christened the "French War Kite," a name that lingers on to this day.

With two simple modifications, you can give the Conyne an "airplane" look.

On the left, the Conyne becomes a delta wing when the spar is placed across the base and framing strings are drawn to the tops of the spines. The kite at right, if built with a 3'-long skeleton, should have wings spanning out 2' to either side. Each tail extends out a foot.

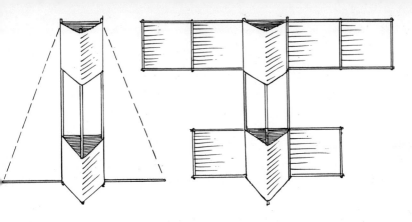

Conyne Kite as an airplane

For the last three chapters, we've been very busy at your worktable. In all, you've had the chance to build eleven flat, ten bow, and ten box kites. More building lies ahead, with the most unusual of kites yet to come. But let's take a breather for a while. How about going outside for a flying session?

7

FLYING YOUR KITE

All the chapters that have gone before have been leading up to this moment—the moment when you carry your kite out through the front door and release it to the wind. It is a moment that will mark the start of many pleasant and exciting hours. The true flier can think of no time more fascinating than that spent guiding his handiwork through its dance in the sky. Somehow, even though his feet never leave the ground, he is a pilot, right up there with his "plane."

As you ready yourself for this, your first flight, you've probably got four questions uppermost in mind. Is this a good day for flying? Where can I best fly the kite? How do I get it into the air without trouble? And what do I do with it after it's there? The purpose of this chapter is to help you learn the answers. We'll get to them in a moment.

But for now, before you head out the door, think of more immediate matters. Make sure that you have all the necessary accessories. Remember, you'll need a knife, some extra string, and a few pieces of cloth for bridle and tail adjustments. You might also take along a small roll of transparent tape in case the cover tears. And add to your list an item of equipment not mentioned before—a reel for your flying line.

The Kite Reel

As is true of all other kiting equipment, the reel is the simplest of devices. Any spool-like object will do, so long as it is large enough to accept the full length of your line. A stick, a dowel, a section of branch, a piece from a broom handle, a cardboard tube, or even a tin can—take your pick. Each will serve well. Just keep one point in mind: Make sure that your choice is a bit on the thick side. Hauling in a kite can be a wearying job for the hands and wrists if the reel has a small core.

Many fliers today use short fishing rods with reels attached. If you have the money for it, a rod-and-reel will prove a good purchase, for the rod magnifies the movements of your arm and gives you a greater control over the kite. Such a rig, however, can run on the expensive side, so why don't you see if someone has a spare one that you can borrow. Perhaps a friend or a second-hand store has one for sale at a bargain price.

With a few minutes work, you can land midway between a plain old stick and a fancy rod-and-reel. Try making your own reel, one complete with handles. Homemade rigs are not only serviceable but good-looking.

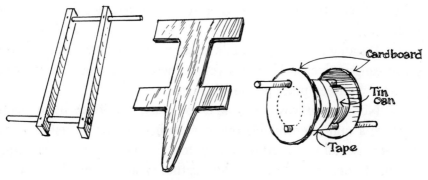

Homemade kite reels

When to Fly

Once outside, look at the day around you. Is it clear and bright? Is the sky empty or perhaps whitened here and there with a few clouds? Is there a steady breeze of a velocity somewhere between four and eighteen miles an hour? If so, you're set for a flying session. The weather conditions are just right.

On the other hand, if the clouds threaten a storm or if the wind is up over twenty miles an hour, you'd best wait for another day. Benjamin Franklin survived a storm, but you might not be so lucky; electricity, from lightning or a power line, passes through wet strings and cords far faster than through the air. A wind above the twenty-mile-an-hour mark is getting too heavy for most kites. Paper starts to tear. Strings break.

Wind velocity is your single most important flying condition. It will even determine the kite that you choose for the day. Most small, lightweight kites do well in winds of 4–6 mph. Conventional-sized kites can handle winds in the 7–18 mph range. Sturdy, heavy-duty models are needed for winds 18–20 mph. If the day is warm, humid, and partially cloudy, that's the time to bring out your best highflier. The weather suggests the presence of thermals, which are rising bodies of warm air. If your kite finds one, it's in for a speedy climb of several hundred feet, followed by a fine high-altitude flight.

It's all well and fine to talk about wind velocities. But how do you gauge velocity? How can you tell whether a breeze is running nine or fourteen miles per hour? By guess?

No. If you wish, you may purchase an inexpensive wind gauge; a quite dependable one can be had for just a few dollars. Otherwise, all you need do is look to see what the breeze is doing to the things around you. Is the weather vane on a neighbor's roof turning? Is dust swirling along a roadside? Are leaves rustling in the trees? According to a system of wind identification known as the Beaufort Scale, all are clues to certain velocities. For instance, the Scale will tell you that:

1. A breeze that is felt lightly on the face, that rustles tree leaves and moves an ordinary vane but fails to keep a small flag flying has a velocity of 4–7 mph. It is classified on the Beaufort Scale as a "light breeze."

2. A breeze that puts small tree leaves and twigs into motion and extends a small flag is blowing at 8–12 mph. The Beaufort Scale classifies it as a "gentle breeze."

3. A breeze that disturbs small branches and raises dust and loose papers is blowing at 13–18 mph. It is classed as a "moderate breeze."

4. A breeze that causes small trees in leaf to sway and forms crested wavelets on a lake has a velocity of 19–24 mph. Its classification is "fresh breeze." Take out your sturdiest kite.

5. A breeze that whips large branches about, that sings in power lines, and that pulls hard at umbrellas is running in the 25–31 mph range. It's called a "strong breeze." Best to stay home and read a book. Or build another kite.

The Beaufort Scale was developed in 1802 as an aid for seamen and is named for its British inventor, Rear Admiral Francis Beaufort. It describes conditions observed in anything from a dead calm to a hurricane, but the five descriptions given above are the only ones that you will ever need as a flier. They'll answer that question uppermost in any kite man's mind at the start of the day: Is there enough wind for the kite that I want to fly?

If you're at all in doubt about wind strength, just take your kite outside and, holding it by the bridle, lift it a little above your head. Should the breeze catch the kite and set it at a flying angle, you can get ready for a flight. The wind is strong enough for the day's work.

Where to Fly

A kite may be sent aloft anywhere outdoors, but two words should always be your guide when choosing a spot for flying: open space. Obstructions—trees, power lines, and roof tops—are everywhere and always seem ready to grab at any passing kite. Stay as well away from them as you can.

A hilltop, a meadow, a pasture, or a stretch of prairie will be an ideal choice if you live in the country. Should your home be near the ocean, hurry down to the beach and take advantage of that fine offshore breeze. If you're a city dweller, look for a park, a playground, a schoolyard, or even a tennis court. Your own yard, front or back, may be fine if it offers enough space and is well clear of obstructions.

Obstructions. They're the bane of the kite flier's life. You not only have to watch for trees, power lines, roof tops, flagpoles, and TV antennae, but also keep an eye out for hedges, fences, and even holes in the ground. Your kite can easily dive into a hedge or fence when landing. You can back into either all too easily while concentrating on the job at hand, or stumble in a small hole. So, give your surroundings a close look at the start of every flying session. Avoid all the obstructions possible and take note of the locations of those that can't be avoided. While you're at it, make a promise to stay clear of roads and your local airport, not only for your own safety but for that of others as well. A suddenly dipping or diving kite can distract, startle, or panic a passing driver. And high-flying kites have long been recognized as a danger when flown within the landing patterns for aircraft.

A very wide berth, of course, must be given to power lines. You already know just how dangerous they are to the flier. Further, there is always the possibility that your snagged kite will "black out" a section of town. Should your kite ever be caught in a power line, don't throw sticks or rocks at it or attempt to tug it free. Above all, don't climb after it and don't let any of your friends with a monkey complex try to do so. Break the string and hope that the kite blows free or falls away of its own weight. If it stays where it is, leave it and, though it may break your heart, write it off as a loss.

Much the same goes for roof tops and trees. Don't climb to the kite's rescue; no matter how agile you may think you are, climbing is a risky business. Unless the line or the tail is hopelessly snagged you may be able to fly the kite off a roof top or out of a tree. Say that the line is caught on a branch or beneath the edge of a shingle; try to "walk" the string free, shift around until your back is to the wind, and then wait for a friendly gust to lift the kite away. If luck runs against you, you have no choice but to pull the kite away. You'll likely ruin it, but at least you'll know that you protected some youngster from coming along later and scrambling up after it.

Trees have the bad habit of catching a kite in their small upper branches. If you must pull the kite down, do so gently so that you will not damage the young limbs. In fact, do all that you can not to damage or disturb any of the natural life around you. Plants, flowers, bushes, trees, spider webs, animal nests, and the animals themselves—all should be protected and left in peace. They all live there, and every good kite flier knows that he is just a guest. So act accordingly—please.

Flying Your Kite: The Launch

You may think that you must always launch your kite on the run. The running launch, while sometimes necessary, is actually frowned upon by most fliers today. All too often, they say, it ends in failure, with the runner tripping over some obstacle or the kite diving into the ground after swinging wildly from side to side.

Most kites can be sent aloft from a standstill. Some will rise directly from your hand.

The launch directly from your hand is delightful. Nothing is more satisfying than to see the wind pluck at the kite and carry it right away from your outstretched fingertips. For such a launch, stand with your back to the wind and raise the kite up in front of you, holding it by the bridle and at arm's length. When you feel a healthy gust, release the kite with a slight toss. The wind will do the rest. If you're working with a rod-and-reel, cast the kite out in front of you at the right moment.

Once the wind has caught the kite, begin to pay out the flying line. Let out the line as steadily as possible, but take care not to release too much at one time, for then it will go slack, the kite's angle of attack will "flatten," and you'll lose lift and flying control. Keep the line taut at all times, perhaps taking a few steps backward to help matters along. The stronger the wind, the faster you'll be able to feed out the line.

You'll need to help matters along by tugging downward on the line. Downward tugs give additional altitude by pulling the line to an angle more vertical to the ground. The tugs—sometimes they need to be no more than mere twitches—also do much to keep the kite head up and facing into the wind. Any kite is in its greatest danger during the launch and landing. Here, it is most apt to dart wildly from side to side or nose over into a dive. The danger stems chiefly from the fact that you are working with a short line. It permits a minimum of movement to one side or the other before the kite is flying at an angle to the wind rather than riding before it. Tugs at the right moment will save you many a crash.

Incidentally, should the wind be a trifle on the light side, you'll be wise to hold the kite somewhat out to your side just prior to launch. Otherwise, your body might block off the amount of air flow needed for lift.

If the wind is strong enough, there is hardly a reason why you cannot hand launch any small or conventional-sized kite, whether it be a flat, a bow, or a box. With a very light wind, though, you'll probably have to turn to the distant launch. Again, you'll be able to launch from a standstill.

Suppose that you have a friend along as a helper. Send him about one hundred feet downwind and have him hold the kite up and angled into the wind. With the first strong gust, he's to signal you with a yell and release the kite. In the same instant, you're to reel in the line a few yards. This has the same effect as a downward tug, and the kite should shoot skyward, hopefully catching a firm breeze that will support it. Now, by alternately tugging at the line and letting it out a few feet at a time, you coax the kite higher and higher until it's truly flying.

If you're by yourself, you can still launch from a distance while standing still. When readying a flat or bow kite for flight, let out a few yards of line and place the kite face down on the ground. Pull the line gently so that the flat kite raises its face to catch the wind. With the bow, simply stand with the line held loosely in your hand; the wind should get under the curved face and lift it. If the kite has a tail, be sure to lay the tail line straight out on the ground *toward* the wind. When the kite rises, the tail line will then flow up under it and not be dragged along the ground behind it.

The distant launch for the box kite is handled somewhat differently. Stand the kite on end and back off a few yards. Then tilt the box forward by pulling gently on the line. As the kite tilts, the wind should pick it up and smoothly lift it clear of the ground.

Flying Your Kite: Aloft

Unless the wind is very steady, you're going to do far more than just stand there, gawking skyward and holding onto the flying line once the kite is aloft. There will be those memorable times when the kite seems "to fly itself," but on most days you're going to be kept busy making all the corrective movements necessary for sustained flight. You'll be tugging at the line, letting a bit out reeling a bit in, and changing your position from time to time. But all this is part of the fun of kiting. You really *are* the pilot, up there and in control.

Let's look at a few of the things that may happen and see what you can do about them. Sometimes a kite will rise beautifully to a certain altitude and then refuse to travel higher. The chances are that it has found a layer of calm air. Ordinarily, there is another layer of moving air just a short distance above, and you can usually coax the kite up and into it by releasing a stretch of line and trying a few short tugs. You'll know when the kite is free of the calm. It will pull and usually begin to rise.

Incidentally, as the kite rises out of the ground wind and ascends through the layers above, don't be surprised if it shifts about somewhat. The upper winds usually move in directions different from that of the ground. You may see the line curving out in different directions. The curves indicate the various layers of air and the paths of their travel.

In a light breeze, the air pressures at the front and back of the kite may equalize. Instead of filling with air as it should, the cover will flap and the kite will begin to sink. This is called "luffing" (the same term applies to the ship's sail when it goes limp) and it can usually be cured by steadily pulling in on the line until the kite again catches the wind. If you build your kite with a taut cover, you'll reduce the chances of luffing.

While the wind can play all sorts of tricks on you, most control problems arise from the kite. Fortunately, most can be easily remedied.

An incorrectly placed tow point accounts for much difficulty. With the point set too high along the bridle, the kite will lie too flat for efficient flight, although it will probably remain aloft in a light breeze. If the towing point is too low, the kite will be top-heavy and will insist on diving, looping, or darting wildly from side to side. Whatever the case may be, adjust the tow point accordingly and send the kite up for a test flight. But exercise a little patience. Adjust the tow point no more than an inch at a time. You'll avoid overcompensating and will find the correct point all the sooner.

The tow point is just one of several potential troublemakers. A skitterish kite may need longer bridle legs so that it can meet the wind with greater flexibility. A kite that persistently darts to one side most likely has bridle legs too short on that side. The box kite that is unsteady probably has its cells too close together.

The bow kite that performs sluggishly or wants to dive because it is top-heavy should have the depth of its bow reduced; a more shallow bow will provide greater lift. The flat kite that rises with difficulty, with its tail line hanging low rather than flowing out horizontally behind it, needs to have the tail line shortened. If the kite dances up and down, the tail line should be lengthened. A too-short tail line may also put the kite into a dive or a loop.

Incidentally, there's no danger in a dive or a loop at a high altitude. Both are exciting to see and are used by stunt fliers. But close to the ground—they'll stop your heart, for they promise a shattering crash. Whether at a high or a low altitude, let the flying line go slack when the kite dives. At a high altitude, the kite will likely end the dive in a lateral loop, at which time you can bring it head-up and into the wind with a series of tugs on the line. At a low altitude, should the kite end up on the ground, it will strike with less force if the line is slack.

Your flight problems can be many and varied. But never let them discourage you. A little experience and know-how will enable you to identify and correct them all. As said before, practically all can be easily solved. And, remember, all are a part of the fun and challenge of kiting. One of the great satisfactions is to adjust the misbehaving kite and then watch it perform to perfection.

RANGED DISTANCE TO KITE, OR LENGTH OF LINE (YARDS)

Angle (degrees) to kite	100	150	200	250	300	350	400	450	500	750	1000
05	8	13	17	22	26	30	34	39	43	64	86
10	17	26	34	43	52	60	68	78	87	128	174
15	25	39	50	64	78	90	100	116	129	193	250
20	35	51	70	85	103	120	140	153	170	256	340
25	42	63	84	105	126	147	168	190	211	316	422
30	50	75	100	125	150	175	200	225	250	375	500
35	57	84	114	142	169	199	228	256	286	428	570
40	64	95	128	159	190	223	256	285	320	480	640
45	70	106	140	176	212	247	280	318	350	528	707
50	77	115	145	191	230	268	290	345	383	574	766
55	81	123	162	204	246	286	324	378	406	612	810
60	86	129	172	216	259	303	348	389	430	648	860
65	90	136	180	226	273	317	360	408	451	678	906
70	93	140	187	234	279	328	374	422	470	704	940
75	96	144	192	241	288	338	385	434	482	724	965
80	98	147	196	246	295	344	393	442	492	738	980
85	99	149	198	247	297	347	396	446	495	744	990
90	100	150	200	250	300	350	400	450	500	750	1000

B

A

C

Altitude of kite (yards)

Angle (degrees) to kite

Flying Your Kite: Altitude

Every flier wants to know how high his kite has traveled. But, as any experienced kite man will tell you, the determination of altitude is a difficult business, one in which there is great room for error.

If you can afford a height finder, you can sight it up your line and obtain an altitude reading quickly. But a finder costs money, and so you'll probably want to depend on what is known as the "range chart." A small graph, it can be carried to your flying grounds and consulted whenever necessary.

Before you are able to use the chart, though, you'll need to make two calculations. First, you'll have to determine just how much line you've paid out. This can be done by sending the kite out to the very end of a known line length or by marking the line at, say, twenty-foot intervals beforehand and then counting the marks as the kite rises away from you.

Second, you'll need to gauge the angle at which the kite is flying. Once the angle and the line length are known, the chart will give you the altitude. As seen above, the chart is divided into three sections. Section A lists the line lengths in yards, while Section B lists the flight angles in degrees. Section C consists of the altitude readings. All you need do is read down from one line length in A and across from one angle in B. The number in C that corresponds to both is your altitude.

The range chart will not give you the most accurate reading in the world when the kite is hanging low with its line bellying out. But as the kite travels higher, straightening the line and steepening the angle to the ground, your calculations will become increasingly accurate. In all, whether the kite is flying low or high, you may miss the actual altitude by a few feet one way or the other. But a miss of a few feet is better than not knowing at all.

Flying Your Kite: The Landing

When it's time to go home, reel the kite in slowly and steadily. This may take a little patience, but a fast reel-in is likely to cause the kite to dart and plunge—a business that grows riskier the closer the kite comes to the ground.

In a light breeze, you'll probably be able to bring the kite to you without taking a step. Just reel in, let the line go slack at the last moment, and allow the kite to drop lazily to the ground a few yards from you. Once the kite is down, walk over to it and pick it up. Don't drag it to you, for the possibility of damage by rocks, twigs, and prickly weeds or grass is great.

In a strong wind, your best bet is to "walk," or "underrun," the kite in. Either plant your reel in the ground or hand it to your helper and then walk toward the kite for perhaps fifty to a hundred feet, passing the flying line through your fingers or under your arm. At the end of your walk, start back toward the reel, this time pulling the kite in as you go. Repeat the process until the kite is down, with your helper winding up the slack line—a job that you'll need to do later if you're by yourself. You'll find that just before landing, the kite is almost directly above your head. With luck, you can bring it right to your hand.

Incidentally, it's always a good idea to wear gloves while flying. They'll prevent many a cut and nick, especially during launch and landing.

Once you're home again, store the kite carefully in a safe and dry place. Keep it out of harsh light so that its fine bright colors won't fade. If it is a bow kite, remove the bowstring, sticks, and framing strings—the cover will then remain resilient for a longer time. If yours is a collapsible box kite, break it down and roll it into a neat package.

8
ADDING TO THE FUN

After you've flown your kite for the first time, you may want to do no more with your hobby than just fly again and again. For many a kite flier, the enjoyment of standing out in the open, manipulating a kite, and watching it hover and dance in the blue is more than enough to satisfy the spirit. But others like to add to the fun by trying special flying techniques, flight accessories, and kite games.

Perhaps you'd like to join them . . .

Special Flying Techniques

If you've built several kites of the same type, you're ready right now to try the easiest of the special flying techniques:

FLYING IN TRAIN

Flying kites in a train is an interesting technique, especially so because it enables them to gain a greater altitude than when sent aloft singly. One type of flex-wing kite (Chapter 9), for instance, has achieved a height of 17,000 feet in train. Its maximum altitude alone is around 9,000 feet.

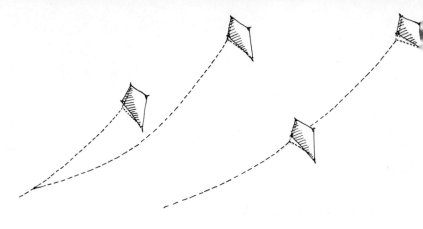

Methods of train-flying

Any strongly built kite may be flown in a train. As indicated above, however, you should limit each train to kites of just one type. And you should take care to increase flying-line strength as the train lengthens. Each new kite exerts an added pull, and if you're not careful, you'll spend a part of the day hunting for the various "cars" in your broken train.

As shown in the illustration, a kite train may be launched in either of two ways. In each case, you'll be wise to have a friend along as a helper. Train-flying is really a two-man job.

The method shown at left is the simpler of the two. You and your helper should each launch a kite. Let your kite ride out about two hundred feet, while your helper's travels for up to half that distance. Then tie the two flying lines together, cut away the remainder of your line, and, now using your helper's line as the flying line, let the kites out for another hundred feet. Attach the third kite and let the train out farther, this time with the third kite's line serving as the main line. Continue the process until all your kites are aloft.

The second method is considered a more efficient one, but it also requires a degree more flying skill. The first kite is sent aloft. Its line is then attached to the spine-spar intersection of the second. The same point of attachment is used for all other "cars" that follow. The train is apt to jump about a bit as each new kite is released; careful line-handling will get it back "on the track."

You may fly as many kites as you wish in a train. No one really knows how many have ever flown together, but there are stories of giants that have gone aloft with as many as a hundred "cars."

TANDEM-FLYING

If you have two box kites of the same size and design, you may link them together and fly them in tandem. As shown in the illustration, they are usually joined together by an arrangement of crosspieces and bracing strings.

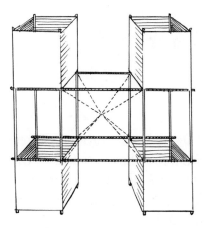

Box Kites in tandem

The box kite, as you know, is a very stable flier. It becomes even more stable in tandem.

KITE-FISHING

Do you like to fish? If so, you might take your kite along on your next trip to the lake or seashore. Wedded to your fishing line, it will combine two of the world's most pleasant sports.

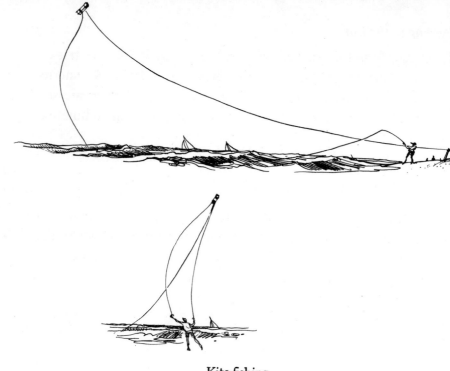

Kite-fishing

Like the top figure in the diagram, try flying your kite out over the water, with a long line attached to the base of the spine. The line extends down to the water and is connected there to your fishing line. The kite flies staked into the ground, leaving you free to handle the fishing rod.

This method is particularly liked by surf fishermen. The kite carries their bait out beyond the breakers, enabling them to fish at a distance impossible to reach by simply casting.

Suppose that you want to troll. Then, like the bottom figure in the diagram, attach two bridles and flying lines to the kite. By working one line and then the other, you'll send the kite sailing back and forth above the water, dragging the baited line behind it.

Should you want to try your hand at kite-fishing, plan to be at the water's edge in the morning. At that time, your chances are best for a wind blowing out from shore.

Westerners learned the art of kite-fishing from the peoples of the South Pacific. Though we here in the United States kite-fish mostly from shore, the above two methods will also work from a boat. When using the first of the two in a boat, however, you'll probably be more comfortable without a fishing pole. Rather, let your fishing line out directly from a reel. You'll then have a little more freedom of movement.

STUNTING AND FIGHTING

Little of practical value can be said on paper about kite-stunting and -fighting. Both are advanced techniques requiring a skill that is learned "on the job," a bit at a time as you fly.

One or two points, however, may prove helpful. Among the best stunt kites are the four-celled tetrahedral (Chapter 9) and the small bow kite with a good, taut cover—perhaps one made of plastic. When learning to fly, pay close attention to your arm movements. Some, done automatically and unconsciously, will indicate ways of deliberately putting a kite into or bringing it out of a maneuver. Try your first aerobatics at a high altitude. Dives, loops, and side-to-side runs will do no damage up there, but close to the ground and all the surrounding obstructions—well, that can be a different story.

Kite-fighting is a very popular sport throughout Asia. The objects of the fight are three: to cut an opponent's flying line and send his kite fluttering to the ground, to "lasso" his kite and bring it down, or to tangle your flying line in his and then haul his kite in.

To cut an opponent's line, Asian fliers send their fighters aloft at the ends of flying lines stiffened with a mixture of glue and crushed glass or porcelain. The lines cut sharply when the kites are at last maneuvered into fighting positions. Some Japanese fliers dangle knives from their kite tails. Looped ropes, also hanging from the tail, are used to "lasso" the enemy and bring him down.

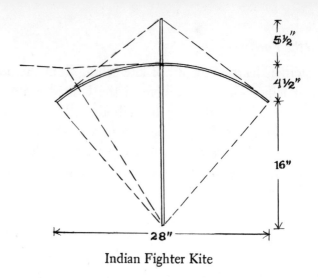

Indian Fighter Kite

Should you want to try your hand at kite-fighting, start with an inexpensive kite, one that you're willing to see ruined within a few minutes. Later, if your interest continues and your skill grows, you may want to build a fighter of your own. One of the finest, the Indian fighter kite, is pictured. A flat kite, it combines the characteristics of all classic fighters—durability and maneuverability. Its skeleton is made of bamboo.

Just one plea: Don't try the Japanese technique of suspending knives from the tail unless you really know what you are doing and have no spectators around. Should one of the knives be cut loose, you'll suffer many a sleepless night if it falls into a crowd.

Kite Accessories

For years now, fliers of every age have used the flying line as a "rungless ladder" to the kite. All sorts of objects have been sent up along its length. Of the lot, the simplest have been:

MESSENGERS

A messenger is nothing more than a stiff piece of paper. You

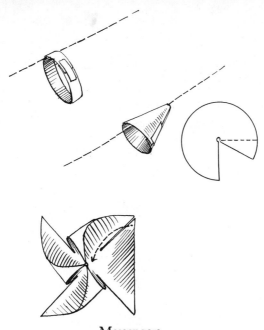

Messengers

simply attach it to the flying line. The wind takes over and sends it up to the kite.

All of us are acquainted with the messenger in its most primitive form. It is a small piece of paper with a hole punched in its center, and a slit running out to its side that enables it to be slipped onto the line. For years, youngsters have enjoyed writing their names and addresses on such a messenger and sending it up the line to be blown free and away. When the messenger is found and mailed to its owner, he'll know just how far it traveled.

Should you wish a fancier messenger, you might fashion any of those in the illustration. The ring is a slip of paper that is looped around the line and then joined at its ends with tape; a dozen or so rings of various colors make an interesting sight when sent up the line one after another. The cone, which is cut in a circle and trimmed as shown, is also wrapped around the line and taped together. Send it up the line nose first.

The pin wheel, however, must be threaded onto the line before launching. Hold it in place, letting the line slide through the center hole, while the kite is being unreeled. When you are read to release the pin wheel, run it out to a point a few feet in front o your reel and give it a spin. The wind will keep it spinnin throughout its ascending journey.

THE MATCHBOX SAILBOAT

One of the most charming accessories is the matchbox sail boat.

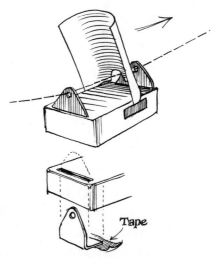

The Matchbox Sailboat

To build, first tape the two triangular supports to the under side of the box cover and then secure the sail by taping its tips to the sides of the box. The sailboat must be threaded onto the line before flight time.

THE PARACHUTE

Equally charming is the parachute, which is made with thread lines, a weight (a metal washer, a stone, or a toy soldier will

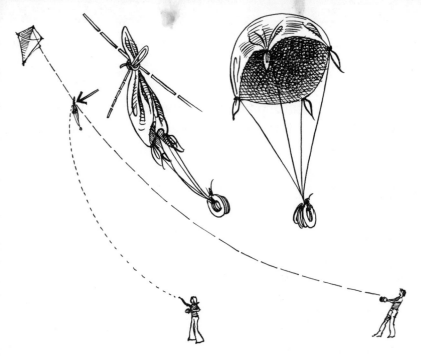

Parachute and string release

do fine), and a canopy of square cloth. It is meant to be sent up the line and then released so that it can float back down. For release, you're going to need an extra line of string.

Attach the parachute with the string, using either a slipknot or a loosely tied bowknot. As the kite ascends, pay out the extra string along with the flying line. When you wish to release the chute, tug gently at the string. The knot will "break" and the parachute will come drifting down.

Some fliers attach a series of parachutes at intervals along the flying line and then release them one at a time. When a number of chutes are all drifting down together, they have the look of a military "drop." A separate release string is needed for each chute.

THE GLIDER

The release string can serve yet another purpose. Try slipknotting a dime-store glider to a box kite that has crosspieces at the top. The string is then pulled, undoing the knot and releasing the glider.

And there is still another use for the string. Mount your camera to your kite and tie the string to the shutter mechanism. A tug of the string will give you an aerial photograph. For the string to work, however, your shutter mechanism must be the sort that is triggered by being pulled downward. Incidentally, set your shutter for a fast speed. Remember, the kite is constantly on the move up there. Who wants a blurred aerial shot?

MUSICAL INSTRUMENTS

Toy wind instruments or small reed pipes may be attached to the kite. When the breeze is up, they'll begin to play and you'll hear them quite clearly.

Kite Games

For the flier with a competitive spirit, there are a number of kite games and contests. During the breezy times of the year your local Recreation Department may feature them in organized competitions. If you're too eager to wait for the department's next "Kite Day," why don't you go ahead and put together a tournament of your own for your friends—perhaps for your fellow students, your youth club, or your Boy or Girl Scout troop. You'll be surprised at how many of your friends will want to participate.

Kites are usually divided into three classes for competitions— flats with tails, bows without tails, and box kites. They may be further divided into "homemade" and "purchased" varieties. Most events are then scheduled so that each type of kite has the chance to compete against others of its type. Some events—for instance, the "pulling contest"—are best limited to just certain of the types. As for the events themselves—well, here is a list to get you started:

KITE DESIGN AND DECORATION

Prizes are awarded for the best-built and the best-designed kites. In the design category, awards can go to various kites—the one most carefully constructed, the one with the oddest shape, the largest, the smallest. Decoration awards might include "most imaginative design" and "most humorous" design. Kites should be eliminated from the design award if they are unable to fly.

ALTITUDE RUN

Place the contestants at the starting line, each with a fixed length of flying line—say, two hundred yards. At your signal, the contestants begin flying their kites. They are usually given from five to ten minutes to send their kites as high as possible. They are permitted to move about while flying, but must return to the starting line when you signal that their time is up. The winner is the highest-flying kite as seen from the starting line.

SPEED RUN

Again, the contestants work with a specified line length, perhaps one hundred yards this time. On the signal "go," they release their kites and send them out to the full line length. On another signal, they stand at the starting line and reel the kites in as fast as possible. The first kite "home" is the winner.

KITE RACE

Line the contestants up at the starting line and have them fly their kites all out to an equal line length. At your signal, they are to run to a distant finish line—a line that is *in the direction of the* kites. The kite that permits the flier to run the fastest while maintaining its height and not fluttering to the ground is the winner.

Kites not only of the same type but of similar size should be flown in the race. Wait until the wind is light before holding the event. With a strong wind, the kites will likely remain aloft and turn the whole thing into a foot race.

MESSAGE RACE

The contestants are to send their kites out to a specified distance—say, fifty or one hundred yards. Each then dispatches a messenger up his flying line. The first messenger to arrive at the bridle is the winner.

The messengers should all be the same size and type. So that they can all be made on the spot, why don't you call for that most primitive one of all—the square of paper with a hole in its middle and a slit out to its side?

TIME RUN

Contestants send their kites aloft for a given period of time, usually five minutes. The winner is the kite that remains aloft the longest during that time.

This contest should be divided into two events—one for small kites and one for larger kites. If you have a wide variety of kite sizes competing, you may have to divide it even further.

PULLING CONTEST

This competition, which measures the pull of the kite, is best limited to box kites, with the flying wedge always being a top competitor. The kite exerting the most pull on the line is declared the winner.

The amount of pull can be gauged with a small spring scale.

Or you can simply hang a weight from the line about a foot from the reel.

LIGHT-BREEZE RUN

Kites are sent up in a very light breeze. The one that flies the best for five (or ten) minutes is declared the winner.

You'll probably need a wind gauge to determine wind velocity. And you might have to divide the contest into categories—light kites vs. light kites, and average-size kites vs. average-size kites.

POND OR RIVER RUN

You can hold this even only if you're lucky enough to live near a pond or river. Kites are launched across the water, from one bank to another. Each then tries to tow a small log or a long stick back to the flier. The one that succeeds in the best time is the winner.

It's a good idea to send the kites across the water with their tail lines weighted down with a stone. Then a helper attaches the log or stick for the run back.

KITE BATTLES

A kite battle is an exciting contest for both beginners and experienced fliers. The beginners will give everyone—themselves included—a few minutes of high comedy. The veterans will provide a thrilling contest. Unless a great deal of time is taken in preparation, you probably won't be able to coat the lines into "cutters," so why don't you just try dangling lassos instead; of course, stay clear of knives. And you'd best warn all beginners that they're likely to go home with broken kites.

"BOMB" RUNS

This contest runs kite-fighting a close second for excitement. A circular target is outlined in the center of the field. The kites are sent aloft singly with one or more small paper bags filled with flour. The bags are connected to the tail or the flying line by lengths of string, as are parachutes. Once the kites are in position, above the target, the strings are pulled and the bags released. The most accurate "bomber" is the winner.

All these are but a few of the events that you can schedule for your tournament. To the list you might add competitions for hand launches, running launches, stunts, fast climbs, and train flights.

Your tournament should be carefully prepared. All contest rules should be written down so that they can be clearly explained to the contestants at the start of each event. Several of your most level-headed friends should be appointed judges; calmness and fairness are vital in any judge if arguments over contest results are to be avoided. And, of course, you'll need prizes. Ribbons of different colors—say, blue for first place, red for second, and white for third—will do just fine. Simple though they may be, you'll find them enough to bring out the spirit of competition in any flier.

So put your organizational skills to work. You can be guaranteed of one thing: You and your friends will have a day of fun.

9

EAST AND WEST—
A FOLIO OF KITES

As you become an expert kite man, you will very likely want to join those thousands of your fellow enthusiasts who like to build and fly kites of an unusual design. If so, this closing chapter is especially for you. In it, you will find ten of the world's more distinctive kites—four from our own lands here in the West and six from the Orient. All will challenge you as a builder. All will delight you as a flier.

First, Kites of the West . . .

The Checkerboard

MATERIALS

1. Two flat spines, $\frac{1}{4}'' \times \frac{3}{8}'' \times 72''$
2. Four flat spars, $\frac{1}{8}'' \times \frac{3}{8} \times 12''$
3. Cover material and working equipment

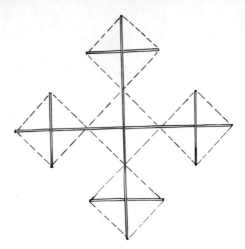

The Checkerboard

If you're interested in scaling your kites to a giant size, you might start with the simple-to-build checkerboard. It performs best when built quite large.

Lash the two spines at their mid-points and then add the spars, placing them 12" from the spine tips. All sticks, of course, should cross each other at right angles.

The skeleton is then to be framed as shown in the illustration, after which the five squares formed by the framing string are to be covered. The kite will be ready to fly when the spars have all been bowed to a 2" depth, and the spines to 6". The bowstrings for the spines should be tied together at their point of intersection.

A four-leg bridle is needed; let the legs come from each of the spar-spine joins. The kite, which flies as a diamond, should be able to do without a tail if properly balanced and proportioned.

The checkerboard is a particularly attractive kite when each square is given a cover color of its own, or when the color used for the outer squares contrasts with that chosen for the center.

The Tetrahedral Kite

MATERIALS

   1. Six framing dowels, ³⁄₁₆″×36″
   2. Cover material and working equipment

   The tetrahedral—that brainchild of Alexander Graham Bell —qualifies as a box kite. Usually called simply the "tetra," it consists of sticks arranged in one or more triangular cells. Though seen in the illustration in its one- and four-celled versions, the kite can be expanded to contain as many cells as you think practical.

   To build the one-celled tetra, shape the framing dowels into a pyramid with all its sides 35″ long. Next, cut two triangular cover panels and then complete the kite by cementing them to the upright sides. The tetra is flown with a two-leg bridle attached to the top and bottom of the covered framing dowel.

   The four-celled version is made by first drilling a hole midway

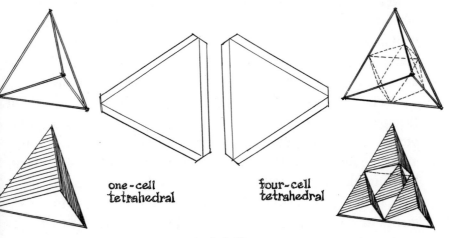

one-cell
tetrahedral

four-cell
tetrahedral

Tetrahedral Kites

along each stick and then forming the interior triangles by passing a string from hole to hole. Make certain that the holes are cleanly drilled since the string will need to pass through each twice.

Complete the kite by covering its various triangles as shown in the illustration. Again, a two-leg bridle is used.

The tetra is a very steady flier, but requires a strong breeze for best performance. Just one caution: Take care as you continue to add cells. The larger the kite grows, the heavier it becomes and the greater the drag it exerts. When too big, it will defy you to get it off the ground unless you have a powerful launch vehicle. Remember Bell's "Cygnet." It required a steamship to pull it aloft.

The Scott Sled

MATERIALS

1. Three dowel spines, $\frac{3}{8}'' \times 36''$
2. Cover material and working equipment

The Scott Sled is an individual unto itself. Named for its inventor, Frank Scott, and for the fact that it resembles a snow sled when aloft, it is a bow kite without a single bowed stick in it. It contains three spines, but they provide little support and are there mainly to give the kite shape. And unlike all other bow kites, it does not fly with its bow arched into the wind but away from it.

The sled may give you a little trouble at launch time when it struggles with the ground wind, but, once it catches a steady breeze, it will balloon out and fly quite stably. Whenever handling a sled, be sure always to keep the line taut. A slack line will invariably cause the kite to "fold in" on itself and begin to flap.

To build the sled, begin with the cover, cutting it to the dimensions shown in the illustration and razoring out the triangular

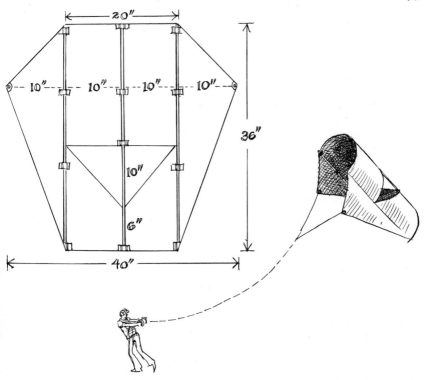

The Scott Sled

vent in its face. Then cement the spines into place as indicated and further firm them down with strips of tape. Tape should be run all around the perimeter of the kite to reinforce the cover, and bridle holes should be punched at either wing tip.

You'll need to experiment to find the best bridle length. A too-short bridle pulls the wing tips too close to each other. A too-long bridle allows them to spread too wide and lose their stabilizing value.

Should you ever want to vary the size of the sled, think twice. It has been built and flown in several sizes, but it invariably performs best with spines 3' long.

The Flex-wing Kite

MATERIALS

1. One sheet of strong paper 18″ square
2. Working equipment

For a truly "spineless" kite, try the flex-wing. Since it needs neither spine nor spar, it can be built in minutes. Along with the Scott Sled, it might prove a bit headachy to launch at first, but once in the air, it will prove a sturdy and dependable flier in a wide variety of winds. It might well become your pet kite.

Begin by reinforcing the edges of the paper with transparent tape or folding them over into 1″ flaps and cementing them down (if you fold the edges, be sure that you start with a larger cover sheet, one that will end up at 18″ square). Next, run a strip of tape down the center of the paper (again, for reinforcement) and then crease the paper firmly along the center line of the tape.

From now on your job is one of bridling. Starting 7½″ from the top of the kite, four bridle holes are to be punched along the center line at 3¾″ intervals. Next come two holes along each edge of the upper sides; they're to be punched 7½″ and 13″ from the top. Finally, two holes are needed along the lower sides; they should be made 7½″ from the bottom of the kite. All holes should be strengthened with transparent tape or reinforcing rings.

Finish off your work by bridling the kite with eight legs each 13″ long. Extend tail lines 20″ long from the two holes near the bottom of the kite. The tail lines should be joined at their ends with one or two crepe streamers about 15″ to 20″ long.

The flex-wing is a distant relative of the parachute and is often called the "parawing." Invented in the 1940s by Francis M. Rogallo of the United States, it is one of the latest innovations in kite design. The parawing design has been used in the airplane

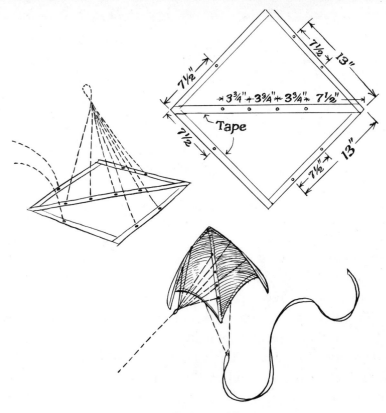

The Flex-wing Kite

and the glider and as a parachute for space vehicles returning to earth.

And Kites of the East . . .

The Cambodian Snake

MATERIALS

1. One dowel spine, $\frac{3}{16}'' \times 14''$
2. One dowel spar, $\frac{3}{16}'' \times 14''$
3. One dowel base, $\frac{1}{8}'' \times 10\frac{1}{2}''$
4. One bamboo framing strip, $\frac{1}{8}'' \times 36''$
5. Cover and tail material; working equipment

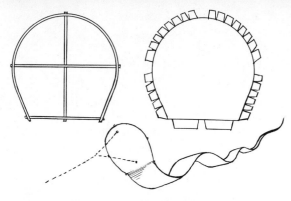

The Cambodian Snake

The first of our oriental kites is the Cambodian snake, with its distinctive, tapering tail. The tail, flowing out behind the kite and rippling in the breeze, makes the snake one of the steadiest and most graceful-looking of fliers.

To build the kite, first mark all four sticks at their centers and ¼″ in from their tips. Additionally, mark the bamboo strip 10½″ to either side of its center. These marks will make the work of positioning the sticks and bending the bamboo to its proper lashing points all the easier and will help you avoid the danger of a misshapen frame.

Glue and lash the spine and spar together at their mid-points, setting them at right angles to each other, after which the base is to be attached to the spine. Set the mid-point of the base on the spine's ¼″ mark. Finally, attach the mid-point of the bamboo strip to the ¼″ mark at the top of the spine and bend it so that it can be lashed to the ¼″ mark at the spar and base tips.

Fashion the cover shown in the illustration, cutting the overlap into tabs about 2″ or 3″ wide along the curves so that it will fit neatly over the bamboo strip. After cementing the cover in place, glue the tail to the base dowel. The tail may be cut to a taper either before or after gluing. Try about five or six feet of paper or lightweight cloth for the tail.

The kite is usually flown with a two-leg bridle. The legs are attached to the spine 2½″ from the top and 3¾″ from the bottom.

The Caterpillar Kite

MATERIALS

1. Seven bamboo framing strips, ⅛"×48"
2. Fourteen dowel braces, ¹⁄₁₆"×16"
3. Cover and tail material; working equipment

The caterpillar kite is sure to dazzle your friends, just as it has been dazzling the people of Asia for centuries. It consists of a series of disks connected by lengths of string. The disks ripple as the wind strikes them, giving the impression of a great caterpillar inching its "up-and-down" way through the sky.

Your first job of course is to fashion the disks. Shape each bamboo strip into a circle and reinforce it with two crossed bracing dowels. As shown in the illustration, each circle may be completed in either of two ways—by overlapping the ends of the strip, or by shaving the ends into points whose flat sides meet.

Cover each circle with a paper disk. Let each cover have a 1" overlap that is divided into tabs 2" or 3" wide for neat folding. The disks are then connected to four lengths of string that run the length of the "caterpillar's" body; the disks should be set at 12" intervals along the strings. Lastly, a tail should be cut to the shape shown in the illustration and attached to the seventh disk.

The kite is flown with a two- or four-leg bridle. The front disk is usually painted with a happy face. Alternately placed disks of green and silver give a fine "caterpillar" effect. Reeds from a broom add a nice effect if attached in small clusters to either side of each disk.

The kite may be transformed into the traditional Chinese dragon, one of the largest of kites flown in the Orient, by making each disk successively smaller all along the length of the body.

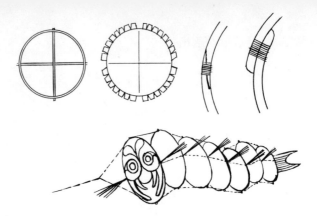

The Caterpillar Kite

Though seven disks have been used here, you may add as many as you wish to the caterpillar or the dragon. Some dragons run to a length of fifty feet or more and require a team of men to get them into the air.

The Flying Lamp Shade

MATERIALS

1. Three bamboo framing strips, $\frac{1}{8}'' \times 35''$
2. Six dowel braces, $\frac{1}{16}'' \times 11''$
3. Three bamboo spines, $\frac{1}{8}'' \times 36''$
4. Cover material and working equipment

The flying lamp shade is an especially popular kite in China. It combines the three dimensions of the box kite with the circles that form the disks in the caterpillar kite.

The circles are built as they were for the caterpillar kite, with the skeleton then being completed when the spines are attached, as shown in the illustration.

Cover the kite just as you would if it were a box kite, drawing the paper taut as you go and cementing it to each spine in turn. Leave about 1″ overlap and fold it back over the circles at the top

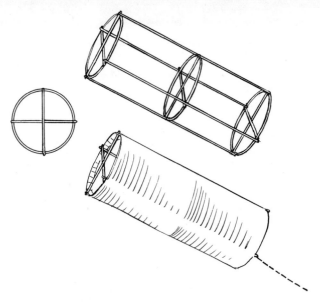

The Flying Lamp Shade

and base, cementing it into place. You'll need to cut the overlap into tabs 2″ or 3″ wide for a neat fold over the circles.

The kite can be flown with a one-leg bridle attached to the base of one of the spines. The lamp shade does not require a tail.

For decoration, why don't you try spacing oriental language characters or boldly painted clusters of bamboo shoots on either side of the cover?

The Orange Kite

MATERIALS

1. Four bamboo framing strips, $\frac{1}{8}″ \times 36″$
2. One flat spine, $\frac{1}{8}″ \times \frac{3}{8}″ \times 46″$
3. Cover material and working equipment

The disk motif continues in the orange kite. At a glance, the kite may seem to have a complicated structure. A closer look

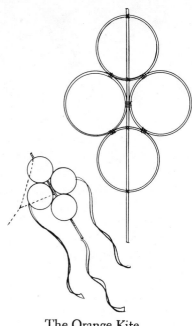

The Orange Kite

shows that it is one of the simplest of the oriental kites to assemble.

All that you need do is shape the four bamboo strips into disks and then, setting the first of their number ½″ down from the top of the kite, attach them to the spine, as shown in the illustration. The disks should be covered *after* attachment. The cover material, of course, cannot be folded back over the bamboo at the points where the disks meet. Cement it to the front of the strips at those points.

Attach a two-leg bridle just above the tops of the upper and lower disks. A tail line, fastened to the base of the spine, will be needed. If you wish, you may add a crepe streamer to the side or bottom of each outer disk.

The cover is usually orange in color, and each disk may be decorated with an oriental language character.

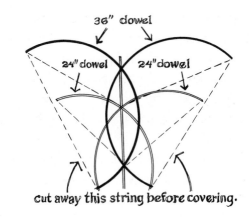

cut away this string before covering.

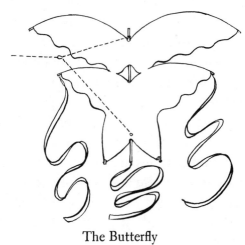

The Butterfly

The Butterfly

MATERIALS

1. One flat spine, ⅛″×⅜″×36″
2. Two dowel wings, ³⁄₁₆″×36″
3. Two dowel wings, ³⁄₁₆″×24″
4. Cover material and working equipment

One of the most charming kites to come from the Orient is the butterfly. It is also one of the more challenging to construct, and so must be approached with great care and patience.

First, each wing dowel must be made into a bow by drawing a string between its tips. The bowed wings are then attached to the spine, as shown in the illustration. The two 36″ dowels are pictured in solid black.

Once the members are all lashed and glued together, two new strings need to be added; they are represented by the dotted lines in the illustration. When they are in place, you can cut away the strings originally used to bow the 36″ wing dowels. With these outer strings gone, the kite now assumes its butterfly shape.

When covering, fold the paper over the tops of the dowel wings and over the curving dowels and framing strings at the bottom of the kite, but leave the lower edges of wings free to flutter in the breeze. Razor out the diamond shape in the center of the face.

The kite is flown with a two-leg bridle. Both legs are attached to the spine—one at the top of the upper wing, the other at the point where the framing strings intersect near the base.

The butterfly is a flat kite and so will need a tail. Try using three crepe streamers, making each about twice the length of the kite and tying them to the ends of the lower wings and the spine.

The Tree Kite

MATERIALS

1. One flat spine, ¼″×⅜″×40″
2. Three tree sticks—two 11″ long, one 5″ long (all ⅛″×³⁄₁₆″)
3. Three tree sticks—two 15″ long, one 7″ long (all ⅛″×³⁄₁₆″)

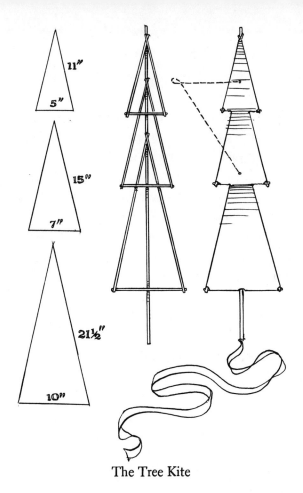

The Tree Kite

4. Three tree sticks—two 21½" long, one 10" long (all ⅛"×³⁄₁₆")
5. Cover material and working equipment

For the last kite in our folio, let's turn again to nature—this time to the tree kite. A favorite in the rural areas of Asia, it is sometimes called the "pine tree" kite, sometimes the "Christmas tree" kite.

To build, first shape each set of tree sticks into a triangle, as shown in the illustration. Next, starting at the top of the kite, lash each tree component to the spine, inserting each of the lower ones beneath the one above. Insert each to about one-third its length.

When all are in place, glue and tie them together at their cross points.

Cut the cover to the shape of the kite, leaving a ¾″ to 1″ overlap, and then carry the paper down the front of the kite, cementing it into place as you go. Attach a two-leg bridle, with the legs coming in from halfway down the top triangle and from a quarter of the way down the base triangle. A tail will be needed.

The kite is usually decorated to resemble a tree. A trunk runs up the spine, with suggestions of branches and leaves extending out to its side. You might want to add a bit of color by painting in a few Christmas tree ornaments.

From one kite man to another:

Good building, good flying, and good fortune.

RECOMMENDED READING LIST

If you're interested in reading more about kites and their construction, the following books will prove both entertaining and valuable:

BRUMMITT, WYATT. *Kites.* New York: Golden Press, 1971.
BURKHART, TIMOTHY. *Kite Folio.* Berkeley, Calif: Double Elephant, 1974.
DOWNER, MARION. *Kites: How to Make and Fly Them.* New York: Lothrop, Lee and Shepard, 1966.
HART, CLIVE. *Your Book of Kites.* London: Faber and Faber, 1964.
HUNT, LESLIE L. *Getting Started in Kitemaking.* New York: Bruce, 1971.
JUE, DAVID F. *Chinese Kites: How to Make and Fly Them.* Rutland, Vt.: Charles E. Tuttle, 1967.
KETTELKAMP, LARRY. *Kites.* New York: William Morrow, 1959.
NEWMAN, LEE SCOTT and HARTLEY, JAY. *Kite Craft.* New York: Crown, 1974.
SAITO, TADAO. *High Fliers:* Colorful Kites from Japan. Tokyo: Japan Publications, 1969.
WAGENVOORD, JAMES. *Flying Kites.* New York: Macmillan, 1969.

INDEX

Edward F. Dolan, Jr. was born and educated in California, and has lived in that state for most of his life. After serving in the 101st Airborne Division during World War II, he was chairman of the Department of Speech and Drama at Monticello College, Alton, Illinois for three years. While writing books for young people, he spent seven years as a free-lance writer in radio and television, and was a teacher for some years after that. His first book was published in 1958 and he has averaged a book a year since then, while continuing to do free-lance magazine writing and editorial work.